Cambridge Elements

Elements in Global China
edited by
Ching Kwan Lee
University of California-Los Angeles

CHINESE GLOBAL ENVIRONMENTALISM

Alex L Wang
University of California-Los Angeles

Shaftesbury Road, Cambridge CB2 8EA, United Kingdom

One Liberty Plaza, 20th Floor, New York, NY 10006, USA

477 Williamstown Road, Port Melbourne, VIC 3207, Australia

314–321, 3rd Floor, Plot 3, Splendor Forum, Jasola District Centre, New Delhi – 110025, India

103 Penang Road, #05–06/07, Visioncrest Commercial, Singapore 238467

Cambridge University Press is part of Cambridge University Press & Assessment, a department of the University of Cambridge.

We share the University's mission to contribute to society through the pursuit of education, learning and research at the highest international levels of excellence.

www.cambridge.org
Information on this title: www.cambridge.org/9781009571760

DOI: 10.1017/9781009363976

© Alex L Wang 2026

This publication is in copyright. Subject to statutory exception and to the provisions of relevant collective licensing agreements, with the exception of the Creative Commons version the link for which is provided below, no reproduction of any part may take place without the written permission of Cambridge University Press & Assessment.

An online version of this work is published at doi.org/10.1017/9781009363976 under a Creative Commons Open Access license CC-BY-NC 4.0 which permits re-use, distribution and reproduction in any medium for non-commercial purposes providing appropriate credit to the original work is given and any changes made are indicated. To view a copy of this license visit https://creativecommons.org/licenses/by-nc/4.0

When citing this work, please include a reference to the DOI 10.1017/9781009363976

First published 2026

A catalogue record for this publication is available from the British Library

ISBN 978-1-009-57176-0 Hardback
ISBN 978-1-009-36401-0 Paperback
ISSN 2632-7341 (online)
ISSN 2632-7333 (print)

Cambridge University Press & Assessment has no responsibility for the persistence or accuracy of URLs for external or third-party internet websites referred to in this publication and does not guarantee that any content on such websites is, or will remain, accurate or appropriate.

For EU product safety concerns, contact us at Calle de José Abascal, 56, 1°, 28003 Madrid, Spain, or email eugpsr@cambridge.org

Chinese Global Environmentalism

Elements in Global China

DOI: 10.1017/9781009363976
First published online: January 2026

Alex L Wang
University of California-Los Angeles
Author for correspondence: Alex L Wang, wang@law.ucla.edu

> **Abstract:** This Element examines China's embrace of green development on the global stage, or "Chinese global environmentalism." It traces Chinese global environmentalism's historical evolution and motivations and analyzes its deployment through the governance tools of green ideology, diplomacy, economic statecraft, and international development cooperation. It conceives of Chinese global environmentalism as a wide-ranging economic and political strategy used to unsettle traditional views of China and bolster the legitimacy of Chinese power at home and abroad. This Element argues that Chinese global environmentalism, while not without its fits and starts, is enabling China to make inroads internationally with implications for China's rise and the natural environment that are only beginning to be appreciated. This title is also available as Open Access on Cambridge Core.

This Element also has a video abstract: www.cambridge.org/EGLC_Wang

Keywords: China, environment, climate change, green development, environmental governance

© Alex L Wang 2026

ISBNs: 9781009571760 (HB), 9781009364010 (PB), 9781009363976 (OC)
ISSNs: 2632-7341 (online), 2632-7333 (print)

Contents

1 Introduction   1

2 Chinese Global Environmentalism: Origins & Ideology   13

3 Green Diplomacy   29

4 Green Economic Statecraft   47

5 Green Development Cooperation   58

6 Conclusion   71

   Bibliography   74

1 Introduction

A decade into the Xi Jinping era, China has become a full-throated proponent at home and abroad of what it refers to as "green development" (*lüse fazhan*). Until recently, it would have been common to hear Chinese officials explain why China was not yet ready to engage in environmental protection or emphasize that developed countries had the responsibility to solve the problem first. It now takes a very different tack on the environment, presenting itself as the "indispensable nation" in environmental affairs – an essential contributor to our most pressing global environmental issues. China's turn towards the environment is evidenced by extensive environmental governance reforms, world-leading manufacturing and deployment of clean energy and electric vehicles, and greater protection of domestic ecosystems that serve as carbon sinks and home to biodiversity. Some have argued that these reforms have allowed China to go from "zero to hero" on the environment (Wang 2020).

This positive image of China as an environmental leader runs up against continuing critiques of China's environmental performance. Despite China's move towards green development, it remains the largest absolute source of many pollutants. This is true for greenhouse gases (GHGs), traditional air, water and soil pollutants, ozone-depleting substances, and more. As Chinese society has grown wealthier, the country's imports of raw materials, soft commodities, and endangered biodiversity have skyrocketed, placing extraordinary pressure on the global environment and resources. As Chinese companies have increasingly "gone global" to invest in infrastructure projects and acquire natural resources in countries around the world, environmental and social impacts have soared. Even as China has moved to address these problems with such measures as a domestic "war on pollution" and a major industrial policy push into clean energy, concerns have emerged about the efficacy and sincerity of China's efforts, the country's illiberal governance style, and the risks of excessive reliance on China for key energy and transportation technologies. More fundamental concerns that green development will enable China to surpass the US and Europe are ever more prominent. These perspectives see China not as a hero but as an existential threat to the natural environment and the existing global order.

This Element examines these debates over Chinese green development and the ways in which China is attempting to shape the discourse to be more favorable to its interests. Green development offers a powerful lens through which to examine China's efforts to bolster its global reputation and to understand the opportunities and challenges China faces in doing so. Green development is becoming an important pillar of China's case that it is a viable alternative to the dominant liberal democratic model represented by the US and Europe, and an indispensable contributor to the good of the global community. This is green development as a wide-ranging economic and political strategy to unsettle traditional views of China and bolster the legitimacy of Chinese power at home and abroad.

China's turn toward green development is being carried out through four overlapping component parts, which I will refer to collectively as *Chinese global environmentalism*. These are: (i) an ideology of Chinese environmentalism, (ii) green diplomacy, (iii) green economic statecraft, and (iv) green development cooperation (see Figure 1).

These efforts are taking place in the context of polarized perceptions of China, its impact on the environment, and its place in the global world order. As this context both informs and is being shaped by Chinese global environmentalism, this introductory section outlines the most prominent discourses concerning China's relationship with (and impact on) the environment.[1]

Section 2 then offers a brief overview of the historical origins of Chinese global environmentalism, highlighting the iterative way in which Chinese domestic environmental governance and its international environmental

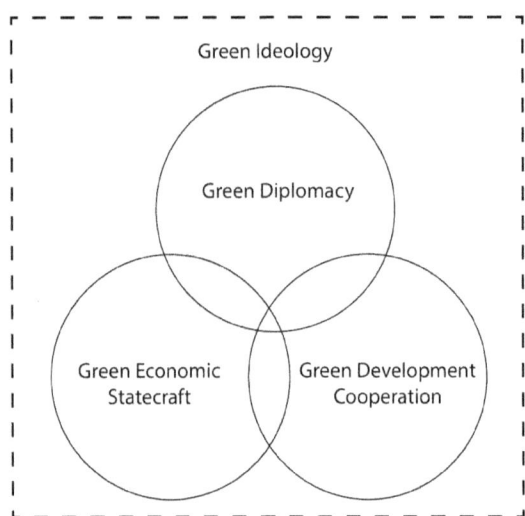

Figure 1 Components of Chinese Global Environmentalism

---

[1] The findings in this section and the rest of this Element are drawn from several dozen semi-structured qualitative interviews in China and elsewhere, a review of primary materials and a burgeoning English- and Chinese-language literature on Chinese global green development, as well as the author's own engagement as a participant-observer in Chinese domestic and global environmental affairs over nearly thirty years.

engagements have evolved over time. This history sheds light on the developmental and political motives that dominate China's environmental moves at home and abroad.

This section concludes by unpacking the characteristics of China's emerging *green ideology* and its close connections to these core Chinese policy objectives of economic development and security. Such an approach has appeal to many audiences in developed and developing countries; however, the developmental focus of China's green ideology also raises important unresolved questions about the relationship of man and nature (or development and the environment) that continue to generate controversy globally.

Section 3 discusses Chinese *green diplomacy* with detailed examinations of the Montreal Protocol and UN Framework Convention on Climate Change (UNFCCC) contexts. In each instance, China can point to actions that support global environmental norms. In other instances, China is actively involved in shaping emerging environmental norms or engaged in vigorous contention over emerging environmental norms. China's move from more defensive positions towards an embrace of affirmative diplomacy and participation in global environmental governance has garnered it accolades. Even so, weaknesses in environmental compliance and tensions over political rights and economic and security risks continue to raise concerns in some quarters.

Section 4 examines Chinese *green economic statecraft*. The focus here is on China's efforts to "green" its outbound investment and trade. China has belatedly aligned itself with the global trend against overseas investment in coal plants, eliminating a major contradiction in Chinese overseas investment and its stated commitment to global climate goals. It has also, in a relatively short span of time, become *the* global leader in the manufacture and deployment of clean technologies. These moves can be understood as part of a strategy to gain economically from green industries, to reduce environmental risk, to position China as a supporter of global environmental and sustainable development goals, and to strengthen ties with countries in all parts of the world. The US and EU to varying degrees have come to see China's growing dominance in the manufacture of clean technologies as an economic and security threat that should be countered through strategies of "derisking" or "decoupling." This section also presents a case study of Chinese green development in Chile to illustrate one country's pragmatic response to green competition among the leading global hegemons.

Section 5 discusses the emergence of Chinese *green development cooperation*. This is a rapidly evolving area in which China has moved from being a recipient of Western aid toward acting as a provider of assistance to the Global South (so-called "South–South" cooperation). It includes government, corporate, and civil society initiatives that serve as sites of technical exchange, relationship building, and image shaping. This section presents the cases of the China Council for International Cooperation on Environment and Development (CCICED) and the Belt & Road Initiative Green Development Coalition (BRIGDC), the Kenyan Standard Gauge Railway (SGR), and the Lancang-Mekong Environmental Cooperation (LMEC). The CCICED and the BRIGDC show the evolution of China from recipient to provider of green development assistance. The Kenyan SGR case sheds light on the conditions under which Chinese state-owned enterprises are more likely to respond to local environmental objections to Chinese development. The LMEC case shows how a Chinese-led regional cooperation institution manages environmental controversy over hydropower projects in the context of broader developmental and security priorities.

Section 6 concludes with implications of this study for our understanding of China's rise and the future of the global environment.

Overall, Chinese global environmentalism has developed into a strategy aimed at several key objectives. It is an economic strategy to mitigate environmental risks of Chinese foreign investment and trade, obtain necessary raw materials, and seek markets for domestic overcapacity in clean technologies. It is a political strategy to build closer relations with Global South countries ("South–South" cooperation) and to present China as a peer great power on par with the US and the EU. It is further a legal and normative strategy to reshape international law and global norms in ways that support China's interests. These strands all coalesce as a strategy to shape global understandings of China and bolster acceptance of Chinese power at home and abroad.

1.1 Discourses of Chinese Green Development

China is now seen in an unfavorable light in much of the developed world. Global polling shows highly negative views of China and Xi Jinping in liberal democratic countries (Silver et al. 2022a, 2022b). In the US, nearly eight-in-ten Americans have an unfavorable view of China, according to polling (Huang et al. 2024, 2025). Moreover, 89% of Americans see China as either an "enemy" (33%) or "competitor" (56%) (Huang et al. 2025). While views of China are more favorable in middle-income countries, China still trails the US in favorability even in these countries (Silver et al. 2023). Negative global perceptions are contributing to material consequences for China as other countries increasingly take trade, security, and other actions.

Polls of Chinese citizen satisfaction with the government suggest more stable public opinion in China's domestic context, but this has not stopped Chinese officials and state media from attempting to bolster domestic support by highlighting Chinese global successes and promoting narratives of US decline (Carothers & Freedman 2025).

Enter Chinese green development. The environment is an area in which China has traditionally been seen as a laggard and poor performer, but where active policy engagement, governance implementation, and manufacturing innovation have begun to reshape impressions of China in ways both dramatic and subtle. The struggle over what China stands for with respect to the environment, or its social construction in the eyes of global and domestic audiences, is a central focus of this Element.[2]

In explaining the concept of constructivism in international relations theory, Alexander Wendt famously noted that "500 British nuclear weapons are less threatening to the United States than 5 North Korean nuclear weapons" because "the British are friends and the North Koreans are not" (Wendt 1995, p. 73). In other words, who states are *understood to be* matters in international relations. Consider instead the contrast between Western and Chinese framings of air pollution in China. Western commentators have commonly attributed China's air pollution problems to its authoritarian political system, whereas Chinese experts more frequently treat it as a problem of development stage. Alternatively, consider the different responses to Korean or Chinese electric vehicles in the US. The former are seen as unthreatening export products, whereas the latter are associated with security risks, job losses, unfair trade practices, overcapacity, intellectual property theft, and undue political influence. In each of these examples, we can see who is considered a friend and who is not.

The following section delineates the contours of the debate about China and the environment, including critical and positive perspectives as well as the audiences likely to hold these views.[3] This clarification of discourses will set the stage for our discussion of the history of Chinese global environmentalism

---

[2] Scholars have explored the dimensions of this idea in different conceptual terms. Some have discussed Chinese environmental governance as a source of political legitimacy (Wang 2013, 2018b; Teng & Wang 2021). Others have utilized the idea of "soft power" or the ability to move "others to want the outcomes that you want" (Nye 2004). This is the "ability to achieve goals through attraction rather than coercion" (Nye 2004, p. 5). Several scholars have begun to write about Chinese "green soft power" (Nedopil 2021; Harlan & Lu 2022; Rodenbiker 2023b; Nedopil & Yue 2024). In writing about Global China, Lee (2022) has also drawn on Bourdieu's concept of "symbolic domination" or the "production and reproduction of power through symbolic forms (e.g., art, religion, language, media) due to their ability to construct, name and classify realities, making certain things thinkable, even natural." This is the idea of symbolic domination as one of several "generic power mechanisms" employed by Global China (along with economic statecraft and patron-clientelism). It is sufficient for purposes of this Element to frame the discussion in terms of contestation over different understandings or social constructions of China.

[3] For purposes of this Element, relevant audiences include elite actors and the general public in developed countries, the Global South, and within China's domestic context. Elite actors include political, economic, academic, and civil society elites.

and the mechanisms of the Chinese global environmentalism playbook. It will also help to sharpen our sense of the ways in which China is attempting to reshape understandings of the country globally and at home through its pursuit of green development.

1.1.1 Critiques

Critical constructions of China and the environment have evolved over time with shifting emphasis as China has become more serious about (and more capable at) tackling its environmental problems. These are perspectives that the Chinese state has sought to counter or neutralize.

Weak Policy Formulation and Implementation. A prominent and long-standing critique holds that infirmities in China's governance model hinder effective environmental policy formulation and implementation. Mao promoted the idea that "Man Can Conquer Nature" (*rending shengtian*) and China proceeded largely in defiance of the natural world in the early decades of the People's Republic of China post-1949 (Shapiro 2001). Maoist China's abuse of nature was closely linked to the political system's abuse of people. This seeming disregard for the environment continued under the Reform Era push for economic development at all costs, despite ever more frequent official policy pronouncements of support for the environment (Smil 1984; Economy 2004). In a study of Chinese climate governance prior to the Xi era, Gilley argues that China's environmental governance model was "more effective at producing policy outputs than outcomes" and that a more participatory approach might improve policy formulation and implementation (Gilley 2012 at 295, 298). In some instances, this has been framed more bluntly as greenwashing, or Chinese officials or firms saying one thing but doing another on the environment. This basic concern that China operates without much consideration for environmental priorities has only grown as Chinese companies have increasingly "gone out" into the world in search of natural resources, markets, and investment opportunities (Simons 2013; Economy & Levi 2014).

These accounts have in common a concern about the lack of institutional checks and democratic accountability within China's authoritarian system. Scholars have long associated authoritarian systems with weak environmental protections and seen censorship, limits on political participation and civil society, and corruption as drivers of environmental degradation (Brain & Pal 2019). The logic here is not difficult to understand. Environmental histories in democratic contexts such as the US, Europe, and Japan have emphasized the role of democratic processes, civic demand, or republican moments in bringing about modern environmental regulatory regimes (Schreurs 2009). Where the channels for public participation are limited, one would expect government action to address environmental protection more slowly, if at all. Although scholars have more recently identified cases where developmental or reputational concerns have motivated environmental action in authoritarian states (Brain & Pal 2019), the sense that environmental governance requires a system that responds to democratic demand remains strong.

Weak environmental performance also undermines China's claims to legitimacy from economic performance. If the costs of environmental degradation amount to 6–8% of China's GDP as World Bank studies have found, then Chinese economic growth looks less impressive than advertised (Johnson et al. 1997, p. 23; World Bank & PRC Govt. 2007).

"Bad" Authoritarian Environmentalism. As I will document in Section 2, Chinese officials began to take environmental issues more seriously during and after China's 11th five-year plan beginning in 2006. As officials started to push for stronger environmental governance and to achieve demonstrable policy outcomes, a line of critique has shifted focus to China's "state-led, coercive, authoritarian style" of environmental governance (Li & Shapiro 2020, p. 23). The most sustained argument in this vein has come from Yifei Li and Judith Shapiro in a book entitled *China Goes Green: Coercive Environmentalism for a Troubled Planet.* They say that "there are admirable elements in the decisiveness of Communist Party policy makers on environmental issues, but there is also much to fear." (Li & Shapiro 2020, p. 22). They argue that the "crackdowns, targets and technological surveillance tools used to implement environmental protection are also being used to assert and consolidate the hand of the state over the individual and over citizens groups ... Not only are individual and social freedoms sharply curtailed by China's approach but even the environmental successes are not always what they seem." (Li & Shapiro 2020, p. 23). Examples cited include Shanghai's recycling program, botched implementation of a switch from coal to natural gas in northern China, afforestation by monoculture, forcible resettlement of local populations in the name of ecosystem restoration, and even China's one-child policy. Human rights groups have joined in this criticism of authoritarian environmentalism, arguing that "the Chinese government harnesses its vast surveillance power to enforce environmental rules," and severely restricts "what citizens and civil society groups can say or do" on environmental issues (Wang 2022). Other scholarly accounts in this vein include Denise van der Kamp's (2020) research on China's "blunt force" regulation through which "officials forcibly shutter or destroy factories to reduce pollution, at immense cost to local growth and employment." Under this view, the Chinese government is wielding authoritarian means to achieve environmental ends and is further using environmental goals to justify tighter political control and weakened civil liberties.

As China has prioritized green development and built substantial clean energy industries, newer critiques have emerged concerning the economic and security risks of Chinese green development and the broader geopolitical risks associated with China's rise. I address each of these in turn next.

Economic & Security Risks. China's growing dominance in key clean energy industries – solar, wind, electric vehicles, and so on – has raised concerns over a surprisingly broad range of economic and security risks. These include concerns about espionage, intellectual property theft, job losses, resource competition, risk of geopolitical conflict, supply chain disruption, price shocks, critical infrastructure vulnerability, and dual use (Davidson et al. 2022). The empirical basis for these economic and security risks is hotly contested. Nonetheless, it is beyond dispute that policymakers in the US, EU, and elsewhere have framed clean energy industries as strategic pillar industries that cannot be ceded to China, and have begun to implement a host of tariffs, security measures, and industrial policy initiatives designed to compete with and constrain Chinese green development growth. As further discussed in Section 4, Global South countries, on the other hand, who stand to benefit from strong trade relationships or access to low-cost, high-quality clean energy technologies, have tended to view Chinese green development more as an opportunity than a risk.

Hegemonic Displacement Risk. Underlying these debates over economic and security risks is perhaps a more fundamental concern – that green development will enable China to displace the US as the leading global hegemon. Realist international relations scholar John Mearsheimer has, for example, criticized US engagement policies that "created a geopolitical rival" and argued that the US should have instead begun to check Chinese economic growth early in the Reform Era (Mearsheimer 2021). His basic argument is structural – that the scale of China's population and economic growth will lead to growing military power that the US must counter in some way, by developing more quickly itself or slowing down Chinese growth. On this view, green development is among a group of industries, including quantum computing, artificial intelligence, and semiconductors, that will determine which country dominates the world in the future, economically, technologically, and militarily. Hegemonic displacement risk is of particular concern in "within the Beltway" discourses in the US, but is also salient in other jurisdictions that support or prefer a US-led world order.

1.1.2 Positive Perspectives

These negative critiques are tempered by more positive perspectives that have also evolved over time as China increasingly embraces green development and aligns its domestic political economy with global environmental norms. These sometimes track official Chinese rhetoric but have also developed independently and in relation to the perspectives of particular audiences (e.g., environmental experts and advocates; Global South countries; and actors disillusioned by existing Western approaches to environmental protection).

Developmental Perspectives. One way to understand China's environmental challenges is not as a problem of political model, but rather as a consequence of development stage. The Environmental Kuznets Curve predicts an inverted U-shaped relationship between economic development and environmental degradation. That is, environmental degradation increases with per capita GDP at lower levels of development until a tipping point, after which environmental degradation decreases as incomes rise. This is hypothesized to happen because rising incomes increase public demand for environmental amenities, provide the resources for investment in pollution control, and lead the economy to shift toward less polluting industries (including through pollution export).

Such a view puts less emphasis on political differences and sees China as following a path already trodden by the US, Europe, Japan, and other developed countries in some instances and engaging in governance innovation in others. Once again consider China's air pollution problems. For a time, severe air pollution in China received intense negative attention from the international community, and Beijing became a global symbol of bad air pollution and weak environmental governance. After China's extensive "war on pollution" and a national air pollution action plan, air pollution has improved markedly throughout the country, and Beijing is no longer even in the top 100 of most polluted cities in the world (Myllyvirta & Howard 2018). Beijing's elimination of the "airpocalypse" has become a symbol of Chinese environmental success. Previously a marker of regulatory failure, it will now likely go down in history as a dark yet ultimately fleeting moment in Chinese environmental history and development akin to famous environmental incidents in the US (the 1948 smog incident in Donora, PA or Cuyahoga River fires in the 1960s), England (the 1954 London "fog"), and Japan (Minamata mercury poisoning, cadmium pollution and *itai-itai* disease).

Chinese officials often point out that China has been going through a period of environmental troubles much like what the developed world experienced at earlier stages of development. At times, they have even used the comparison to suggest that China is tackling more serious environmental problems in a shorter span of time than other countries. These arguments gain much of their force from the fact that China is not unique in facing serious environmental consequences of industrialization and is arguably performing "no worse than" or even "better than" its peer rivals at similar stages of development. I elaborate on this idea in the discussion of "relational perspectives" in Section 1.1.3.

"Good" Authoritarian Environmentalism. Chinese global environmentalism also draws on positive impressions of Chinese environmental governance that have emerged in recent years, particularly as China has made some environmental progress and rapidly developed clean energy technologies. An influential view sees China as a productive authoritarian environmentalism characterized by "its ability to produce a rapid, centralised response to severe environmental threats, and to mobilise state and social actors" (Gilley 2012). What's more, given the severity of global environmental degradation, a "'good' authoritarianism, in which environmentally unsustainable forms of behaviour are simply forbidden, may become not only justifiable, but essential for the survival of humanity in anything approaching a civilised form" (Beeson 2010).

Official Chinese rhetoric in the Xi era has emphasized the value of "top-down design" (*dingceng sheji*) and contrasted China's approach with liberal democratic approaches that are seen as excessively contentious or deliberative, too slow, or captured by industry (Qiu 2024). Put another way, China is more able to "get things done" in infrastructure development, manufacturing, and policy implementation than its democratic counterparts. The empirical basis for these claims is hotly contested, but demonstrable Chinese successes in the Xi era (e.g., air pollution reduction, clean energy deployment, high-speed rail) have offered support for this point of view.

China's top-down, state-driven approach to global environmental governance has influenced norms concerning environmental governance globally. This can be seen, for example, in the turn toward green industrial policy in the US and EU. The US Inflation Reduction Act and the EU's Green Deal Industrial Plan have emerged as countermeasures to China's industrial policy push for green development. Particularly in the US, such measures would have been politically untenable in past years. Although Republicans still largely oppose such measures, the success of Chinese industrial policy has dramatically shifted the Overton window on green industrial policy in the US.

Beyond global debates about the merits of authoritarian environmentalism, China's rise has also spawned some intellectual interest outside of China in Chinese ideologies of ecological civilization. Philosopher Arran Gare has, for example, praised Chinese ecological civilization in a series of books and articles (see, e.g., Gare 2017). Anna Lake Zhu has explored the idea of different Chinese notions of environmentalism in a study of Chinese import of rosewood from Madagascar (Zhu 2022). Although these do not reflect mainstream views, they are nonetheless examples of engagement with Chinese ideologies within intellectual communities outside of China that grapple with Chinese ideas as possible alternatives to dominant Western modes of thinking.

Pragmatic Perspectives. Outside of the developed world, China's push for green development has received more nuanced reception. China has become an important source of investment in renewable energy and clean technologies. It is an important export market for countries producing critical minerals and other raw materials necessary to clean energy supply chains. It now manufactures the clean energy technologies and electric vehicles that countries need to meet green development objectives. These contributions to economic growth and clean energy transition offer other countries a pragmatic reason to engage with China and to resist the politicization of China's rise. Even though these investments and economic engagements have not been without controversy in these other countries, they are nonetheless being met with greater openness than in the US and EU. The US and EU have increasingly sought to counter closer Chinese ties in the Global South, warning countries of the risks of Chinese debt trap diplomacy, inadequate environmental protections, weak labor practices, and the like. At least in some jurisdictions, these warnings have not had their intended effect and have been viewed as hypocritical or merely politically motivated, rather than genuine reflections of risks on the ground.

As a structural matter, China's engagement in global green development has also spurred a competition for the favor of Global South countries among China and its chief rivals in the US and Europe. As with so-called "vaccine diplomacy" during the COVID-19 pandemic, Global South countries may garner greater aggregate benefits as the major powers attempt to outdo one another. In the green development context, for example, the US and Europe have competed with China to offer Global South countries greater support for green development and a chance to move up the value chain. Chinese companies have built or offered to build manufacturing or processing facilities in countries that previously only served as sources of raw materials. China has introduced a South–South Climate Cooperation Fund, although the fund has been criticized for disbursing very little since its inception. The US, Japan, and EU countries have countered with programs like the Just Energy Transition Partnership (JETP), meant to facilitate clean energy transition in South Africa, Indonesia, Vietnam, Senegal, and other countries. The US, however, exited the partnership in March 2025 at the beginning of the second Trump administration.

1.1.3 Relational Perspectives

China's reputation is not assessed in a vacuum. There is a relational component as well. That is, Chinese standing is influenced in important ways by how China is seen in relation to its chief rivals, for better or worse.

Western observers may take some comfort in studies showing that China remains less popular than the US in much of the world. Pew polls have shown a more than 50 percentage point difference in favorability ratings of the US and China among those surveyed in the US, Japan, South Korea, and Poland and more than 30–40 percentage points in western European countries, Canada, Australia, India, and Israel (Silver et al. 2023). Allan et al. (2018) have argued that "China is unlikely to become the hegemon in the near term" because, unlike the US, it is not backed by an ideology that appeals to elite and mass audiences within major countries. The four critiques of China described previously have all arisen in contexts where China is seen as inferior to Western models of rule (e.g., democratic, rights- and market-oriented) as a matter of values or performance.

I nonetheless argue though that China's standing may be enhanced in at least three potential ways connected to how China is seen in relation to its competitors.

First, China may simply gain in standing by performing better than its rivals in tackling environmental problems. China's dominance in clean technology manufacturing and deployment is an example of an area in which China is making gains relative to the US and Europe (see, e.g., Lewis 2012; Gallagher 2014; Nemet 2019; Nahm 2021).

Second, China may get a boost in standing if its rivals begin to perform worse than expected. The Trump administration's multiple withdrawals from the Paris Agreement and aggressive attacks on renewable energy and electric vehicles, for example, give China an easy opportunity to present itself as a global climate leader, despite extensive criticisms of China's absolute level of emissions, continued domestic expansion of coal-fired power plants, and shifting of emissions abroad.

Third, China may be viewed in a more positive light if its actions are seen as "no worse than" what the US and other rival countries have done. It matters, for example, that the US, European countries, and Japan all experienced similarly dire bouts of pollution and environmental degradation during the most intense periods of industrialization. Chinese green development may be seen as a more viable alternative to dominant Western notions of sustainable development despite its imperfections if sustainable development is also seen as fraught with contradictions or problems. It makes a difference if Chinese companies are performing no worse than developed country multinational corporations on environmental impacts in global investments.

Alternatively, China will arguably need to do more to enhance its global standing if its chief rivals are performing well on the environment or achieving results in ways that the relevant audiences find preferable.

* * * * *

Table 1 Discourses of China and the environment

Negative discourses	Positive discourses
Weak policy formation & implementation	Developmental perspectives
"Bad" authoritarian environmentalism	"Good" authoritarian environmentalism
Economic & security risks	Pragmatic perspectives
Hegemonic displacement risk	
Relational perspectives	

The various perspectives discussed earlier are summarized in Table 1. Relational perspectives can temper or strengthen the effect of any of these other discourses on Chinese standing. China's efforts to promote green development play out against this backdrop.

We next turn to a brief history of domestic developments that presage Chinese global environmentalism. The picture that emerges differs from both official Chinese narratives and the more critical takes on Chinese environmental governance. Rather, what we find is a fragmented and imperfect process that has nonetheless moved incrementally over time toward the achievement of some environmental policy goals while falling short on others. This history sets the stage for a discussion of the emerging ideology of Chinese global environmentalism.

2 Chinese Global Environmentalism: Origins & Ideology

In May 2019, I found myself at a toxic soil remediation site in the far western Chinese municipality of Chongqing. The site was operated by a subsidiary of Sinochem Corporation, one of the largest chemical companies in the world. Nestled among rolling hills near the banks of the Yangtze River in the town of Fuling, the site was a showcase for the increased priority of environmental protection under Xi Jinping. Prominently placed on top of a mountainous waste pile in characters the size of the Hollywood sign was a phrase that could be loosely translated as "green is gold (see Figure 2)." This is *the* key slogan associated with Xi Jinping's concept of *ecological civilization* and the company was making it clear that the signals from Beijing had been well-received.

When I first began working on environmental issues in China in the late 1990s, this sort of remediation site would have been unimaginable. In a rural place like this, local government officials would have had little interest in environmental protection amidst the country's relentless push for economic

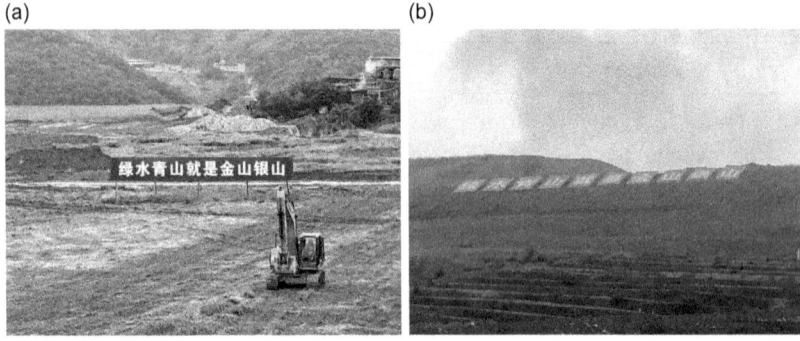

Figure 2(a) and 2(b) "Green is Gold (*lüshui qingshan jiushi jinshan yinshan*)," Fulin District, Chongqing (May 2019, author photos).

growth. If we were able to speak to local villagers, their stories would often sound in hopelessness: damaged crops, cancer villages, unchecked pollution, and unresponsive local officials.

The remediation site here was meant to signal a new Chinese direction on the environment. Billboards highlighted some forty high-level visits to the site from central and provincial Party and government officials, suggesting the importance of the site as a showcase for China's environmental turn. Our small group of "foreign experts" touring the site was in Chongqing to speak at a regional training for Chinese judges on legal methods for handling soil pollution disputes. The very fact that judges were engaging in discussions on such technical environmental issues suggested that China was in a more environmental place than even just a few years before. The following history seeks to explain this evolution.

2.1 China's Long March toward Green Development

State legitimacy and the natural environment have long been connected in Chinese governance philosophy since as early as the Western Zhou Dynasty (1045–771 BCE). Natural disasters, like floods, droughts, and earthquakes, were seen as signs that the Heavens were dissatisfied with a ruler and that the ruler was losing the "Mandate of Heaven" (Zhao 2009). Environmental problems thus were associated with dynastic collapse and could bolster the position of those seeking to rebel against existing rulers. The collapse of the Tang Dynasty in 907 CE has been attributed to prolonged drought, a cooling climate, and a weakened monsoon that harmed agricultural output and produced widespread famine (Gao et al. 2021). The Ming Dynasty's end in 1644 CE has been tied to a Little Ice Age, several periods of severe drought, locust plagues, flooding, and volcanic activity that likewise caused famine, infrastructure destruction, and social unrest (Zhang 2010). Given this history, the connection between environmental problems and regime stability cannot be far from the minds of present-day Chinese rulers.

Nonetheless, under the CCP, China paid little attention to environmental protection prior to the commencement of Deng Xiaoping's Reform Era in 1978 (Smil 1984; Shapiro 2001). This was a period of resource-intensive growth driven by Mao-era policy and "output-oriented state planners and production ministries" (Ross 1992, p. 628). Internationally, China participated in the 1972 Stockholm conference, but its interventions at the time were combative and ideological. The head of the Chinese delegation blamed environmental problems on capitalism and US imperialism and focused his public remarks on criticizing US involvement in the Vietnam War. Nonetheless, Chinese preparations for the Stockholm meeting led to the creation of the first Chinese environmental institutions. China's State Council convened a first National Conference on Environmental Protection in 1973 and established a Leading Group on Environmental Protection in 1974 (Xie 2020). But consumed by political turmoil and with a per capita gross national product of only US$75, the environment was simply not a priority during this period (Cai & Voigts 1994).

When the country emerged from the chaos of the Cultural Revolution, China was a broken and impoverished nation and environmental matters were hardly top of mind. In December 1978, the decision of the Third Plenary Session of the Eleventh Central Committee of the CCP marked the commencement of China's post-Mao Reform Era. This was a period of dramatic economic reform and growth averaging more than 10% per annum. Rapid economic expansion brought with it increasingly severe environmental problems. Perhaps surprisingly, construction of an environmental regulatory regime commenced at the very start of this period. Contemporaneous accounts attribute this to elite awareness of the social costs of pollution and ecological damage (Ross 1992). This environmental regulatory activity could also be seen as part of the broader effort at the time to rebuild a legal system and bureaucracy that had been decimated during the Cultural Revolution.

In 1979, the National People's Congress passed a framework Environmental Protection Law. Over the next two decades China would pass environmental laws on marine environmental protection (1983), forestry (1984), water pollution (1984), air pollution (1987), water resources (1988), and water and soil conservation (1991), solid waste (1995), and noise pollution (1997), among others. Nonetheless, these legal authorities tended to be weak with vague and hortatory provisions, and environmental authorities were subordinate players within the bureaucracy with limited power (Alford & Shen 1997).

At the national level, China's lead environmental institution progressively gained bureaucratic status in successive governance reforms but continued to be subordinate to powerful development-oriented actors within the system, such as the State Planning Commission, the Ministry of Finance, and production-oriented ministries. At the local level, environmental protection bureaus faced fundamental limits on their enforcement powers. They reported to development-oriented local governments that controlled their budgets and staffing (Jahiel 1998; Ma & Ortolano 2000). This structural dynamic contributed to persistent local protectionism and weak environmental enforcement within China.

During this period, China made certain advances in environmental protection. The legal, policy, and institutional foundations established during this period would pave the way for later reforms. Indeed, one contemporaneous account called post-Mao environmental reforms "an extraordinary turnaround, dispensing with revolutionary rhetoric in favor of a more pragmatic approach to contemporary problems" (Ross & Silk 1987). Moreover, rapid expansions of light industry and a shift toward greater market orientation led to efficiency increases and reductions in pollution intensity. But China's evolving environmental regulatory regime could hardly keep up with the pace of rising environmental degradation. Although Li Peng declared environmental protection to be a basic state policy in 1983 and senior leaders repeatedly stated that environmental protection should proceed in tandem with economic development, in practice environmental priorities would continue to take a backseat to economic objectives.

The economic focus was hardly surprising, given China's relative poverty and the importance of rapid development to the Party's hold on power. Chinese leaders saw economic development as a key to stability in the wake of Tiananmen Square crackdown and the collapse of the Soviet Union. Underpowered environmental laws and weak environmental regulatory agencies were arguably a feature of the system at this time, rather than a bug. Environmental protection had its supporters at the elite levels, but rapid economic development remained the overwhelming priority.

Internationally, China was active in environmental diplomacy during the first two decades of the Reform Era. Between 1978 and 2000, China acceded to some thirty-one international environmental agreements (Cai & Voigts 1994, pp. S-24; Ross 1998, p. 815). Its early environmental diplomacy was part of an overall effort across issue areas to rejoin the international community and to limit Taiwan's participation in these spaces. China's environmental diplomacy in the early years was in significant part also aimed at fending off limits on development, blocking potential threats to state sovereignty, and obtaining funds and capacity-building assistance for domestic environmental work.

Although China's historical contribution to global environmental problems at the beginning of the Reform Era was limited in comparison to that of the US or European economies, rapid economic growth brought about substantial increases in Chinese emissions of ozone-depleting substances, GHGs, and other pollutants. China's expanding global environmental impacts brought with it greater international scrutiny and Chinese concern about the potential for international restrictions (Economy 1998, p. 270). This led to a push, commencing in the late 1980s, to develop Chinese "environmental diplomacy" (*huanjing waijiao*) and to train a cadre of environmental specialists to take part in international meetings and to represent Chinese interests (Ross 1998).

In 1990, a cross-agency process led to the creation of a set of negotiating principles for Chinese environmental diplomacy. These were, perhaps unsurprisingly, overwhelmingly developmental, although some voices within the system hoped to emphasize China's responsibilities to the international community and the potential for environmental problems to harm China itself. Among the participants in these debates, the Ministry of Foreign Affairs and the State Planning Commission pushed for developmental positions, whereas the National Environmental Protection Administration (NEPA) and the powerful State Science and Technology Commission (SSTC) supported more environmental positions (Economy 1998, pp. 270–272).

China publicly aired its support for these principles at the 1992 United Nations Conference on Environment and Development (UNCED) in Rio. Premier Li Peng's speech at Rio emphasized development and sovereignty. China offered full-throated support for the concept of "common but differentiated responsibilities" (CBDR), which emphasized the role of developed countries in causing global environmental problems and their responsibility to move first and to offer support for global action. The concept of CBDR would also appear in the UNFCCC and in substance in the Convention on Biological Diversity. The principle was reflected notably in the bifurcated structure of the Kyoto Protocol, under which developed countries had binding emissions targets and developing countries, like China and India, did not.

Although China's most pro-environmental actors did not succeed in setting a more environmental agenda for the country at the diplomatic bargaining table, they were highly successful in obtaining funding, technology, and capacity building through environmental diplomacy and international cooperation in this period. These efforts were led by legendary environmental figures like Qu Geping – head of NEPA (1987–1993); Song Jian – head of the SSTC; and Xie Zhenhua – head of China's environmental agency from 1998 to 2005 and later China's lead climate negotiator (Economy 1998).

An early success came from the 1990 negotiations of the London Amendments to the Montreal Protocol, where China successfully pushed for the creation of a multilateral fund (MLF), with China and India receiving substantial amounts through the fund. During this period, China received billions of dollars (USD) in funding from international institutions, including the World Bank, the Global Environment Facility, the Asian Development Bank, and the United Nations Development Program and bilateral sources (Economy 1998). China received 80% of its environmental budget from foreign sources at one point (Economy 1998).

By the turn of the millennium, Chinese environmental protection had made some progress but was still stymied by low political priority relative to the economy, weak laws and institutions, bureaucratic fragmentation, insufficient funding, and limited public participation.

2.2 Initial Moves to Green Development

As China joined the WTO in 2001, it was a country that had experienced unprecedented economic growth over two decades. But this growth also produced extraordinary environmental problems in air, water, soil, and ocean pollution; land degradation, deforestation, and erosion; and biodiversity loss (Liu & Diamond 2005). Environmental devastation generated high levels of economic losses, such as from water shortages, sandstorm damage, agricultural damage from acid rain, and the cost of combatting harmful invasive species. Recognition of the health costs of pollution was growing. An influential 1997 World Bank study examined health, ecosystem, and agricultural costs of air and water pollution, and estimated that environmental costs were 8% of GDP (Johnson et al. 1997, p. 23). Another study put losses from pollution and ecological damage at 7–20% of GDP (Liu & Diamond 2005). Social conflicts due to environmental problems in the form of protests, disputes, lawsuits and the like were on the rise.

In 2001, Chinese leaders introduced, at the highest levels of the system, the idea that environmental concerns could be a potential limit on economic development. In remarks announcing China's 10th five-year plan, Premier Zhu Rongji commented that resource limits (fresh water, farmland, energy, and strategically important minerals) and environmental degradation would limit China's ability to continue in the "crude manner of growth" that the country had embraced in prior decades. These statements are consistent with Jiang Zemin's remarks a few years earlier at the 1996 fourth National Environmental Protection Conference, which marked the first time a top leader had noted that environmental protection "could not be subordinated without affecting long-term development" (Ross 1998). Senior environmental officials like Qu Geping had much earlier called for greater constraints on development in the name of environmental protection, but the idea had now been taken up by China's most senior leadership.

Entry into the WTO would slingshot China's economy to further growth, increasing demand for energy and resources and placing ever greater pressure on the environment. China's economy would grow by more than ten times, and Chinese exports would expand by more than five times in the next fifteen years. During the 10th five-year plan (2001–05), in addition to worsening pollution, China suffered from nationwide power shortages, and, between 2002 and 2005, economy-wide energy intensity (the amount of energy expended to produce a given unit of GDP) increased for the first time since the early 1980s. These developments exacerbated leadership concerns about energy security and ecological limits on development and spurred greater interest in energy efficiency and pollution reduction programs.

During the Hu Jintao-Wen Jiabao administration from 2002 to 2012, officials considered environmental policy under broader Hu-era political framings that emphasized "scientific development" (*kexue fazhan*) and "people at the center" (*yiren weiben*). As a concept, "scientific development" was meant to convey the need for higher-quality, efficient growth, a contrast to the "development at all costs" approach that had been the norm. In the eyes of many within the system, a December 2005 State Council *Decision on Implementing Scientific Development and Strengthening Environmental Protection* (the "Decision") marked a turning point in the priority of environmental protection as a Party-state political priority (PRC State Council 2005). The document was frank in its assessment of China's environmental problems. The official characterization of China's environmental crisis now acknowledged "huge economic losses, threats to public health, social stability and environmental safety" as potential consequences.

The Decision explained the motivations for Chinese environmental policy:

> The strengthening of environmental protection is beneficial to such activities as economic restructuring; transformation of growth mode and better and faster growth; the development of environmental industry and its relevant industries; fostering of new growth engine and increase of employment; the rise of environmental awareness and moral level of the whole society to promote the development of socialist cultural and ideological progress; guarantee of public health, raising living standard and longevity; the long-term interests of the Chinese Nation and pass on a good environment for our future generations.

Released just three months after the Decision, China's 11th five-year plan (2006–11) reflected an "environmentalist worldview," and marked "the first time that the national government has been so strongly committed to the environment" (Naughton 2005). The 11th five-year plan contained for the first time binding environmental and energy targets, instead of non-mandatory guidance targets. These "energy saving, pollution reduction" targets (*jieneng jianpai mubiao*) were designed to promote greater economy-wide energy efficiency and reductions in air and water pollution. In my field research, local officials in multiple cities described this as a turning point on the environment. They openly admitted to ignoring the pollution targets in the first year of the five-year plan (because such targets had never previously been important), but also reported that the central government made concerted efforts over the next few years to signal to local officials that these targets were now to be taken more seriously (Wang 2013).

A panoply of policies and laws emerged during this period to implement the targets. In 2006, the National Development and Reform Commission (NDRC) launched the "Top 1,000" enterprises program to improve energy efficiency at the country's largest companies. The NDRC also announced a ban on inefficient "backward production capacity" (*luohou channeng*) in the most energy-intensive industries, including steel, cement, and non-ferrous metals. China's legislature passed the 2005 Renewable Energy Law, which would lay the groundwork for the subsequent development of Chinese solar, wind, battery, and other clean energy industries.

This was also a period of public ferment over environmental issues, with increased public awareness, burgeoning public protest, an invigorated civil society and growing global attention to China's environmental woes. On the ground, observers noted that the Decision and the 11th five-year plan emerged amidst ferocious sandstorms in Beijing that dumped some 300,000 tons of sand on the capital (Xinhua 2006). Large-scale environmental accidents, like the 2005 Songhua River benzene spill, occurred with regularity. Environmental protests increased by 29% per year between 1996 and 2011 (Kennedy 2012).

Environmental civil society groups experienced a golden age not seen before or since. China's earliest environmental groups, such as Friends of Nature, Wang Yongchen's Green Earth Volunteers, and Liao Xiaoyi's Global Village of Beijing, pushed for conservation of charismatic megafauna and wild places. Others like former reporter and activist Ma Jun and lawyer Wang Canfa brought attention to pollution with Ma's book *China's Water Crisis* and Wang's law school-based legal organization, the Center for Legal Assistance to Pollution Victims (CLAPV). Smaller regional or local NGOs like Yun Jianli's Green Hanjiang, Huo Daishan's Huai River Defenders, Yu Xiaogang's Green

Watershed, and Wu Dengming's Green Volunteer League of Chongqing acted as local monitors of pollution.

Chinese officials experimented with public participation and transparency mechanisms during this period. Laws like the *Administrative Licensing Law* set forth procedural rights to participation in administrative hearings. China's State Council passed a regulation on open government information in 2007, with China's environmental agency the first to create implementing measures.

Despite this progress, a yawning gap remained between "laws on the books" and "law in practice." Local protectionism of industry remained a persistent problem. Local firms and protective government officials colluded on data falsification and looked the other way at illegal dumping. Environmental lawsuits encountered unsympathetic local judges. The 11th five-year plan ended chaotically. Officials reported that environmental and energy targets had largely been met. At the same time, the head of NDRC issued a public apology about widespread cheating among localities struggling to meet their goals (Wang 2013, pp. 421–422, 431). Some officials shut down power to hospitals and stop lights to conserve energy. Firms used highly polluting, off-grid diesel generators to obtain power without registering the energy use in official statistics. China's turn toward the environment had begun, but its initial implementation was fraught.

2.3 The Rise of Ecological Civilization

As the 11th five-year plan concluded and the Hu-Wen administration prepared to step down, it was not at all clear that China would continue to build on its fledgling environmental and climate reforms. Yet, as Xi Jinping ascended to power, China broadened its domestic environmental reforms and took aggressive steps to deepen the ideological and institutional foundations of these reforms under the rubric of ecological civilization. This included expansion of binding environmental and energy targets, a proliferation of new environmental and energy laws and policies, and institutional reforms aimed at centralization of regulatory authority and tightening of enforcement and implementation. These moves suggested that China's environmental measures were more than merely symbolic. Observers have argued that these reforms were motivated by a complex mix of factors, including concerns about continued economic development and energy security, popular demand for reduced pollution, technocratic response to potential impacts of climate change on China, international normative pressures, and a strategic interest in getting ahead of shifts in energy structure and technology demanded by global climate agreements (see, e.g., Boyd 2012; Wang 2018b).

The concept of ecological civilization was elevated domestically through leadership speeches; incorporation into party doctrine, policy, and law; and campaign-style promotion. The concept was folded into core Chinese Communist Party ideology in 2012 with the announcement of the CCP's so-called "five-in-one" development ideology (*wuwei yiti*). This placed the environment on par with economic, political, cultural, and social construction as core CCP objectives. The concept of eco-civilization was added to the CCP Constitution in 2012 and the Constitution of the People's Republic of China in 2018. Moreover, the idea of ecological civilization was linked to overarching CCP centenary goals of achieving a moderately prosperous society (*xiaokang shehui*) and solving extreme poverty by 2021 (the 100th anniversary of the founding of the CCP) and building "a modern socialist country that is prosperous, strong, democratic, culturally advanced and harmonious" by 2049 (the 100th anniversary of the founding of the People's Republic of China (PRC)), with an interim goal to "basically realize socialist modernization" and a "Beautiful China" by 2035. In 2023, China's National People's Congress designated August 15 as National Ecology Day. Each of these moves signaled an increase in the political priority of environmental governance.

Targets. China continued to elaborate on its system of environmental targets after 2011. The 12th five-year plan (2011–15) contained binding carbon intensity targets for the first time. Environmental and energy targets made up half of all mandatory targets in the 13th five-year plan (2016–20). In 2020, Xi Jinping announced China's "dual carbon" (*shuangtan*) targets at the UN General Assembly – goals to peak carbon dioxide emissions before 2030 and achieve carbon neutrality before 2060.

Implementation Measures. The party and government enacted a host of laws, policies, and enforcement campaigns to promote the achievement of these targets. The national legislature amended the Environmental Protection Law and laws on air pollution, water pollution, solid waste pollution, and marine environmental protection. It passed a new law on soil pollution in 2018. The government launched a much publicized "war on pollution" campaign between 2013 and 2016 to implement pollution action plans for air, water, and soil pollution. The CCP designated pollution control as one of three key governance "battles" (*gongjianzhan*) in 2017, along with the battle to reduce major risks (*huajie zhongda fengxian*) and the battle to alleviate poverty (*tuopin*). China would combine bureaucratic targets and tournament-style competition among officials and jurisdictions, campaign-style enforcement, and a blend of legal, economic, and policy carrots and sticks to drive environmental action.

Institutional Reforms. A range of institutional reforms sought to improve governance and signal the increased priority of environmental protection. Several existing agencies were combined to create the Ministry of Environment & Ecology (MEE) as a "superministry" capable of reducing problems of horizontal fragmentation. Bureaucratic reforms aimed to centralize environmental enforcement through central inspection teams, provincial management of environmental monitoring and inspections, and Party-state joint responsibility. Other measures sought to mobilize the bureaucracy to join in environmental governance through high-level leading groups and the recruiting of banking, securities, and other regulators to enforce environmental rules. Yet others increased public supervision through environmental information disclosure and public interest litigation (Wang 2018a, 2018b).

2.4 Ecological Civilization as Ideology

The maturation of domestic environmental policies, programs and institutional capacity has contributed to the emergence of an ideology of Chinese global environmentalism that China has begun to deploy globally. This is a top-down, state-led developmental version of environmentalism that is beginning to put pressure on global environmental norms forged in the US and Europe.

Just days before Donald Trump's inauguration in January 2017, Chinese President Xi Jinping levied a not-so-subtle criticism of the US in a keynote speech at the World Economic Forum in Davos. "As the Chinese saying goes, people with petty shrewdness attend to trivial matters, while people with vision attend to governance of institutions." Moments later, he added: "We should honor promises and abide by rules ... The Paris Agreement is a hard-won achievement which is in keeping with the underlying trend of global development. All signatories should stick to it instead of walking away from it as this is a responsibility we must assume for future generations" (Xi 2017).

The remark was a reference to Trump's campaign promise to withdraw the US from the Paris Agreement, and Xi's point could not have been clearer. China was a responsible nation and a leader on environmental matters. The US was not. Western and Chinese media amplified the message, never mind China's staggering level of GHG emissions or its continued buildout of coal-fired power plants. This marked an intensification of what former Australian prime minister Kevin Rudd has called the "new geopolitics of China's climate leadership" (Rudd 2020).

The official doctrine of Chinese environmentalism has been elaborated predominantly for China's domestic context. A 2022 People's Daily article, for example, spelled out the content of "Xi Jinping Thought on Ecological

Civilization" in some detail.[4] A few things stand out. This is a vision that first and foremost is led by the CCP (rather than the people or private sector). It speaks in civilizational terms; that is, civilizations flourish when ecology flourishes and civilizations have fallen when nature falters. The goal is harmonious coexistence of man and nature, although the exact definition of this remains unclear. This connects Xi Jinping Thought directly to early Chinese notions of "harmony between man and nature" (*tianren heyi*), "the Way (Tao) follows nature," (*daofa ziran*), and "take things in moderation" (*quzhi youdu*). The environment is a source of economic prosperity. Eco-civilization has a notion of *collective justice* because a healthy environment contributes to the welfare of all people. Xi Jinping Thought expressly recognizes eco-civilization as a "profound revolution in development concept" and a radical move away from earlier, coarser concepts of development. It includes a specific call for "coordinated management of mountains, rivers, forests, fields, lakes, grasslands, and sand systems," which has manifested itself within China in the so-called "ecological redline" (*shengtai hongxian*) program – a massive nationwide zoning project. It calls for "systems," "rule of law," and individual action from Chinese citizens to help implement eco-civilization.

Western scholars have begun to theorize ecological civilization in the Chinese domestic context. For example, Hansen et al. (2018) write that "[e]co-civilization is best understood as a sociotechnical imaginary ... constructed as a ... Communist Party led utopia in which market economy and consumption continue to grow, and where technology and science have solved the basic problems of pollution and environmental degradation." Yeh (2022) writes that "[a]s an ideological framework, ecological civilization draws selectively on reductionist interpretations of China's traditional philosophies while maintaining a long-standing focus on economic growth and on the need for scientific and technological solutions to ecological crises ... " Rodenbiker (2023a) states that "the Chinese state wields ecology to shape nature, society, and space." Goron (2018) and Geall & Ely (2018) have made interventions in a similar vein.

---

[4] The article, by the Xi Jinping Eco-Civilization Thought Research Center, sets forth ten key principles and six practical tasks or directions. The ten principles are: (1) adhere to the party's overall leadership over ecological civilization construction; (2) adhere to the principle that civilization will flourish if ecology flourishes; (3) adhere to the harmonious coexistence of man and nature; (4) adhere to the principle that green mountains and clear waters are gold and silver mountains; (5) adhere to the principle that a good ecological environment is the most universal welfare of the people; (6) adhering to green development is a profound revolution in the development concept; (7) adhere to the coordinated management of mountains, rivers, forests, fields, lakes, grasslands and sand systems; (8) adhere to the most stringent system and the most stringent rule of law to protect the ecological environment; (9) adhere to transforming the construction of a beautiful China into the conscious action of all the people; and (10) adhere to the path of jointly seeking global ecological civilization construction (XJPTECRC 2022).

On the global stage, the ideology of eco-civilization is arguably even more abstract and inchoate. Quotes attributed to Xi – such as "ecological civilization is the historical trend of the development of human civilization" or "building a green home is the common dream of mankind" – are typical. In 2023, China's State Council released a white paper entitled *China's Green Development in the New Era*, which discussed China's domestic green development program at length but offered only modest guidance on China's global green objectives. These included "participating in global climate governance," "building a green Belt and Road," and "carrying out extensive bilateral and multilateral cooperation."

From Chinese statements and actions in these spaces, we can nonetheless divine a few broad themes.

First and foremost, Chinese global environmentalism is a developmental concept. It was initially concerned with environmental limits on development and then evolved into an idea of green development as a vehicle for "higher quality growth." The "core idea" of Chinese ecological civilization is Xi's "two mountains theory." While the concept has some historical resonance within China, its international translation – *green is gold* – comes across as purely developmental. That is, the environment is a source of prosperity. One high-profile platform for the slogan was a UN Environmental Program (UNEP) report by Chinese authors entitled "Green is Gold: The Strategy and Actions of China's Ecological Civilization" in which ecological civilization is presented as a Chinese contribution to the UN 2030 Agenda for Sustainable Development (UNEP 2016).

Chinese leaders have incorporated this green rhetoric into Xi-era foreign policy language. Thus, Xi has promised to "make green a defining feature of Belt and Road cooperation" (China's key Xi-era outbound investment strategy) with "cooperation on green infrastructure, green energy and green finance." Green framings mesh seamlessly with China's general foreign policy language about promoting a "community of shared destiny" and providing the world with "shared benefits" and "global public goods." These core concepts are qualified with reference to a hodge-podge of values such as "extensive consultation," "joint contribution," "policy coordination," "infrastructure connectivity," "unimpeded trade," "connectivity," "financial integration," and "people-to-people bonds." This is a gauzy invocation of green values as a way to pursue a broader panoply of positive Chinese virtues.

Beyond this, China continues to position itself as a defender of Global South interests and to characterize the country as "the largest developing country in the world" (PRC SCIO 2021a). This includes continued invocation of the concept of "common but differentiated responsibilities" and the Five Principles of Peaceful Coexistence. These emphasize sovereignty and the right of developing countries to take more time in meeting global environmental goals while also obtaining help from developed nations. These arguments also draw strength from postcolonial discourses that see aspects of Western environmentalism as hypocritical or self-interested (i.e., that Western nations are asking the Global South to "do as we say, not as we do"). Chinese official rhetoric has also begun to emphasize the "civilizational" aspects of Chinese governance through programs like the Global Civilization Initiative, launched in 2023. The ostensible purpose of the initiative is to emphasize the importance of diversity of civilizations and discourses and to suggest that the Western "rules based international order" is only one acceptable approach among others (Xi 2023).

Underlying all of this is the notion that the steadying Leviathan of Chinese state power at the helm of a broader Chinese civilization is essential to achieving the utopian, win-win visions of Chinese global environmentalism.

These ideational aspects of Chinese global environmentalism are spelled out in an ever-growing body of policy and guidance documents (Coenen, et al. 2020; Hale, et al. 2020; Gallagher & Qi 2021). China's strategic aims for its outbound green activities appeared for the first time in the April 2017 document "Guidance on Promoting Green Belt and Road," issued by the Ministry of Environmental Protection (MEP), Ministry of Foreign Affairs (MFA), NDRC, and Ministry of Commerce (MOFCOM), to promote "the ecological civilization philosophy" and to build a "community with a shared future for mankind." Key normative documents concerning China's global environmental governance are listed in Table 2.

The Xi era has also been marked by a growing proliferation of foreign language materials designed to convey Chinese ideas on global environmentalism to international audiences. These ideas are now regularly advanced through leadership speeches at the highest levels, official foreign policy statements, state-run media, and other publications. The four-volume set of Xi Jinping's speeches, *The Governance of China*, published between 2013 and 2022, contains more than two dozen speeches on global and domestic environmental matters. The China Pavilion at annual UNFCCC climate negotiations is replete with books such as Xie Zhenhua's *China's Road of Green Development*, and Zhou Dadi's *Toward a Green and Low-Carbon Future: China's Energy Strategy*. The magnum opus of Chinese outbound messaging may be a 775-page English-language edited volume featuring essays from more than 70 leading Chinese scholars and researchers, entitled *Beautiful China: 70 Years Since 1949 and 70 People's Views on Eco-civilization Construction*.

Overall, the gist of the message is that China's approach to governance and its pursuit of its own self-interest will benefit the rest of the world in developmental and environmental terms. The most powerful idea here remains the notion that Chinese governance can deliver outcomes that other systems cannot. The subtext

Table 2 Chinese green development policies†

Date	Document	Entities
2013	Guidelines on Environment Protection for Overseas Investment and Cooperation 《对外投资合作环境保护指南》	MOFCOM, MEP
2014	Measures for the Administration of Foreign Aid (trial) 《对外援助管理办法(试行)》	MOFCOM
2015	Opinions of the CPC Central Committee and the State Council on Further Promoting the Development of Ecological Civilization 《中共中央 国务院关于加快推进生态文明建设的意见》	CPC Central Committee, State Council
2017	Guidance on Promoting Green Belt and Road 《关于推进绿色"一带一路"建设的指导意见》	MEP, MFA, NDRC, MOFCOM
2017	The Belt and Road Ecological and Environmental Cooperation Plan 《"一带一路"生态环境保护合作规划》	MEP
2017	Environmental Risk Management Initiative for China's Overseas Investment 《中国对外投资环境风险管理倡议》	GFC, MEP, and others‡
2020	Guiding Opinions on Promoting Investment and Financing to Address Climate Change 《关于促进应对气候变化投融资的指导意见》	MEE, NDRC, PBOC, CBIRC, CSRC
2021	Green Development Guidelines for Foreign Investment and Cooperation 《对外投资合作绿色发展工作指引》	MEE, MOFCOM
2022	Guidelines for Ecological Environmental Protection of Foreign Investment Cooperation and Construction Projects 《对外投资合作建设项目生态环境保护指南》	MEE, MOFCOM

Table 2 (cont.)

Date	Document	Entities
2022	Opinions on Promoting Green Development of One Belt One Road 《推进共建"一带一路"绿色发展的意见》	NDRC, MOFCOM, MFA, MEE

† Entity Abbreviations: Ministry of Commerce (MOFCOM); Ministry of Environmental Protection (MEP, 2008–2018); Ministry of Foreign Affairs (MFA); National Development & Reform Commission (NDRC); Green Finance Committee (GFC) of China Society for Banking and Finance; People's Bank of China (PBOC); China Banking & Insurance Regulatory Commission (CBIRC); China Securities Regulatory Commission (CSRC); and Ministry of Ecology & Environment (MEE, 2018–present).

‡ In addition to the Green Finance Committee (GFC) of China Society for Banking and Finance and the Foreign Economic Cooperation Office (FECO) of MEP, involved entities include the Investment Association of China, China Banking Association, and others.

is that a Chinese-style approach to governance – with top-down, technocratic party-state leadership, marketization within bounds, and emphasis of economic over civil rights, among other things – is better suited to deliver these results. While some commentators have argued that China is in a more ideological age with the ascent of Xi Jinping, the global message here is a pragmatic one as old as politics itself – come with me and I will give you the things that you desire.

A central question is what practical role green ideology plays in Chinese global activity. Does it do any real work or is it mere rhetoric? What is clear is that this is a massive effort to transform Chinese thinking about what constitutes "development" and the proper relationship of man and nature. Less resource intensive or polluting forms of growth are now prized in a way that they were not just a few decades ago. Whereas clean technologies are being presented as a "green scam" at the outset of the second Trump administration in the US (US White House 2025), they are seen as desirable "higher quality" development in China (Qiu 2024; People's Daily 2025). The Chinese ideology also neatly creates a framework for China to take advantage of political economy dynamics that play in the country's favor. Thus, China is seeking to escape the middle-income trap by aggressively cultivating advanced clean technology industries. This strategy helps to mitigate energy security risks, reduce strains on the environment and public health, and bolster China's global reputation through contributions to global development and environmental goals. Most of all, it is a strategy for China to capture the benefits of what it sees as an inevitable global transition to clean energy technologies (Boyd 2012).

Yet many questions remain as to what these general principles mean for action on the ground. How will contradictions between man and nature, development and the environment, or China and the rest of the world be resolved in practice? The doctrine of eco-civilization is beginning to have real bite domestically where it is altering China's economic structure, industrial behavior, and land use patterns. However, there is no guarantee that this will continue, say, if the economy falters or leadership changes. Even if ideology translates into praxis domestically, it is likely to play out differently abroad. Might Chinese green ideology, for example, demand greater ecological protection at home, while tolerating greater environmental impacts globally in the name of development or simply due to weaker global governance capacity or concern?

These are the ideational aspects of Chinese global environmentalism and the questions they raise. Our brief survey here of the ideology of Chinese global environmentalism shows at minimum how China would like the world to understand the country's push for global green development. Sections 3–5 examine how the other aspects of the Chinese global environmentalism playbook are emerging in practice. We turn first to China's use of green diplomacy.

3 Green Diplomacy

China's environmental diplomacy offers a useful lens through which to observe the nuances of Chinese strategy over time. We survey two different treaty contexts: (i) the Montreal Protocol and (ii) the UN Framework Convention on Climate Change (UNFCCC).

The Montreal Protocol helps us to understand conditions under which Chinese actors are willing to take on and comply with environmental obligations, both in the initial stages of the treaty's history and with the more recent Kigali Amendment. In many ways the Montreal Protocol has been a positive story for Chinese green diplomacy and environmental performance. Yet recent enforcement problems with certain banned substances (CFCs and HFC-23) offer a more complex picture – for CFCs, sometimes defensive or combative official Chinese responses, along with aggressive enforcement campaigns that appear to have resolved the problem; for HFC-23, domestic policy responses with incomplete resolution to date of illegal emissions likely emanating from China.

In the case of the UNFCCC, we see China's evolution from a more defensive stance – fending off limits on development, asserting sovereignty, seeking capacity-building support and funding – to a more affirmative approach that takes advantage of domestic developments that can also be framed as global contributions. At the same time, the sheer scale of China's environmental impact, persistent enforcement problems, and the illiberal aspects of Chinese governance (information control, constraints on civil society, and the like) raise persistent criticisms of Chinese behavior. China has in turn asserted that a stronger state hand is necessary to control environmental challenges of this scale and to enable the state to innovate in environmental governance and clean energy manufacturing.

3.1 The Montreal Protocol

The Montreal Protocol on Substances that Deplete the Ozone Layer (1987) and its subsequent amendments implement the Vienna Convention for the Protection of the Ozone Layer (1985) by regulating ozone-depleting substances (ODS).[5] The first major class of ODS regulated was chlorofluorocarbons (CFCs), substances widely used in refrigeration, air conditioning, foam-blowing agents, and aerosol propellants. In the 1970s, scientists discovered that CFCs destroyed atmospheric ozone, which acted as a natural barrier to harmful UV solar radiation. Hydrochlorofluorocarbons (HCFCs) were an important initial transitional substitute for CFCs that have subsequently been replaced by hydrofluorocarbons (HFCs). Although HFCs have minimal impact on the ozone layer, they are potent GHGs. The 2016 Kigali Amendment regulates the phasedown of HFCs. Additionally, HFC-22 is a potent GHG that is the byproduct of the manufacturing process for HCFC-22, a common refrigerant.

3.1.1 Constructive Engagement

China ratified the Montreal Protocol in 1991 and, after some implementation challenges, was successful in meeting the Protocol's initial requirements. Under the Montreal Protocol, developing countries such as China have had more lenient time schedules for phasing out relevant substances and are eligible to receive financial assistance through the MLF, consistent with the principle of CBDR.

China's largely positive engagement with the Montreal Protocol illustrates what may be possible when China's economic and institutional interests are aligned with external environmental goals. Chinese industry was motivated to join and comply with the Protocol because "Chinese refrigerators made with CFCs could not be exported to countries that were parties to the Protocol unless China ratified the agreement" (Zhao & Ortolano 2003, p. 711). Technical and financial support and corporate interest in keeping up with changing global standards mattered as well. China's compliance with procedural requirements

---

[5] China has been the world's leading producer and consumer of ODS since 1996 as developed countries ended their production.

on monitoring and institution building was a prerequisite to funding from the MLF. Chinese partnerships with international experts led to regulatory innovations that aided in treaty implementation. This included the creation of an environmental labeling program for refrigerators that helped Chinese companies satisfy European import requirements and a bidding process for MLF fund allocations that prioritized the efficiency with which projects reduced ODS (Zhao & Ortolano 2003, p. 723).

Moreover, the State Environmental Protection Administration, China's environmental agency at the time, saw in the Protocol an opportunity to enlarge its influence within the bureaucracy and seek resources and technologies for Chinese implementation. Chinese leaders also saw in the Protocol an opportunity to burnish China's international reputation, which was in desperate need of rehabilitation in the years after the 1989 Tiananmen crackdown (Oksenberg & Economy 1999, p. 5).

China's emergence as a constructive partner in the Kigali amendment process has also garnered praise. China ratified the Kigali Amendment of the Montreal Protocol, which governs the phasedown of HFCs, in September 2021.

A Chinese foreign ministry spokesman said of the move:

> China has always taken an active and constructive part in global ozone layer governance and the Montreal Protocol process and played an important role in the conclusion of the Kigali Amendment. China has taken concrete steps to implement the Montreal Protocol and eliminated over 280,000 tons of ozone-depleting substances, accounting for more than half of the total amount eliminated by developing countries. China has also cracked down on illegal production and fulfilled its obligations under the Protocol. China will continue to earnestly implement the Protocol and advance global climate and environmental governance (PRC MFA 2023).

The Kigali Amendment featured two levels of developing country obligations. China signed on to tougher obligations with an earlier freeze date of 2024 for halting HFC production and consumption increases and a more aggressive phasedown schedule. India and several Middle Eastern countries agreed to a later freeze date of 2028 and a more lenient phasedown schedule.

China has received accolades for its support for the Kigali amendment and its willingness to work with the US to reach an agreement (Sun & Ferris 2018). As with earlier phases of Protocol implementation, export market pressures explain China's willingness to move aggressively on Kigali. Some Chinese companies had voluntarily begun to shift away from disfavored substances well before the consumation of the Kigali Amendment, and Chinese industrial policy was tailored to support these industries and their transition away from HFCs (Yang 2023). Shiming Yang (2023, p. 89) also credits China's non-democratic political system for filtering out opposition from some quarters and enabling a deal "more progressive than the ODS sector preferred" – arguably an example of authoritarian environmentalism at work.

3.1.2 CFC and HFC-23 Enforcement Problems

These positive impressions of Chinese action on the Montreal Protocol are tempered by international researchers' discovery of substantial emissions of banned CFCs and continued emissions of HFC-23 despite China's agreement to reduce those emissions "to the extent practicable" by the end of 2021 (Yang 2025).

CFCs. In 2018, researchers revealed that global emissions of banned trichlorofluoromethane (CFC-11) had increased after 2012, despite agreement by parties to the Protocol to phase out global production by 2010 (Montzka et al. 2018, pp. 413–417). Since 2006, reported production of CFC-11 had been close to zero. Scientists and advocacy groups attributed the increased emissions to firms in eastern China (Rigby et al. 2019, pp. 546–550). The Environmental Investigation Agency (EIA), a British NGO, found that "the use of CFC-11 in China's rigid polyurethane (PU) foam insulation sector, in particular in the building and construction subsector, is widespread and pervasive" (EIA UK 2018).

The drivers of increased illegal use of CFC-11s are complicated. Demand for foams used as insulation in buildings, appliances, and other products had grown rapidly due to growth in building construction and tightened energy efficiency standards that increased demand for insulating foams. A key CFC replacement, HCFC-141b, was being phased out under the Protocol at that time, and alternatives to CFCs and HCFCs were considered too costly. As HCFCs became less available, firms turned to illegal production of CFC-11s instead. Local regulators in Shandong province were reportedly aware of illegal CFC-11 production but turned a blind eye (Buckley & Fountain 2018). One factory representative disclosed that "[w]hen the municipal environmental runs a check, our local officers would call me and tell me to shut down my factory. Our workers just gather and hide together" (EIA UK 2018, p. 6). Such collusion between local officials and businesses was commonplace in past years but was thought to have been controlled in the wake of Xi's eco-civilization push.

Chinese environmental regulators responded to allegations of illegal production with denials and hedging, as well as vows of "zero tolerance" for illegal production or use of CFC-11. In practice, "[p]olicy announcements, industry reports and court judgments all indicate that the Chinese government cracked down on the illicit trade, even as it kept denying that there ever was a serious problem" (Buckley & Fountain 2021). In 2018–19, China launched multiple inspections with local authorities on foam producers and promised to improve monitoring and enforcement mechanisms (Buckley & Fountain 2021).

These efforts have apparently been effective in stemming CFC-11 production. According to studies, emissions of CFC-11 declined in 2018–19 and returned to pre-2013 levels in 2019. Park et al. (2021), for example, conclude that "any substantial delay in ozone-layer recovery has been avoided, perhaps owing to timely reporting and subsequent action by industry and government in China." Even highly critical sources agreed that a "nationwide enforcement effort by China in response to the findings appears to have had immediate impact" (EIA UK 2022, p. 4).

What inferences should we draw from the CFC emissions case? On one hand, the case represents the persistence of local protectionism within China and the difficulties of monitoring a relatively unconsolidated industry with numerous, dispersed small and medium enterprises (Yang 2025). The fact that initial accountability for these illegal emissions came from international researchers raises questions about the sufficiency of China's environmental governance. China's regulatory response – initial denials coupled with strict subsequent enforcement campaigns and international cooperation – sends a mixed message to global observers. The incident was undoubtedly a black eye for China's reputation, but subsequent crackdowns and emissions reductions also show China's ability to regulate effectively when alerted to a problem or pushed to do so.

HFC-23. China is the world's leading emitter of HFC-23. HFC-23 is a potent greenhouse gas produced as a byproduct of HCFC-22 production, the interim substitute for CFCs under the Protocol, and a feedstock for other chemicals. Existing technologies can effectively eliminate HFC-23 emissions at relatively little cost through incineration. Destroying HFC-23 is an inexpensive way to eliminate GHGs at large volumes.

China has taken a host of measures to address HFC-23 emissions. In 2013, China obtained US$350 million in funding from the MLF to phase-out HCFC production. As part of this funding agreement, China agreed to "coordinate with stakeholders and make best efforts to manage HCFC production and associated by-product production in HCFC plants" (e.g., destruction of HFC-23) (EIA UK 2013, p. 18). In 2015, China required the abatement of HFC-23 emissions for all new HCFC-22 capacity and from 2014 to 2019 provided subsidies to existing HCFC-22 producers to operate HFC-23 destruction facilities (IGSD 2024). China reported in 2018 that "abatement of HFC-23 emissions from HCFC-22 production reached 99.8%" (Adam et al. 2024).

Under the Kigali amendment, which China ratified in 2021, China was obligated to reduce HFC-23 emissions "to the extent practicable." This has been interpreted to mean that Chinese HCFC-22 producers were immediately under obligation to destroy HFC-23. China's environmental ministry released key documents in 2021 and 2023 that banned direct emissions of HFC-23 and required disposal and monitoring of the substance (IGSD 2024).

Despite these measures, studies have found a persistent HFC-23 emissions gap, with atmospheric measurements showing far greater emissions than countries have reported. An August 2023 study by international researchers found that top-down estimates of HFC-23 emissions based on measurements taken in Gosan, South Korea showed a continuous rise in emissions from 2015 to 2019 that "was contrary to the large emissions reduction reported under the Chinese [HCFC] production phase-out management plan." (Park, et al. 2023). The study authors take the position that these emissions are "more likely associated with known HCFC-22 production facilities" in eastern China and that "the discrepancies between top-down and bottom-up emissions could be attributed to unsuccessful factory-level HFC-23 abatement and inaccurate quantification of emission reductions" (Park et al. 2023). Moreover, the elevated concentrations at Gosan continued after the Kigali Amendment's ban on direct HFC-23 emissions went into effect. A December 2024 study updating these results found that top-down monitored global emissions of HFC-23 in 2023 were five times higher than the most recent bottom-up reported data from 2021 and that China accounted for roughly a third of that global discrepancy (Adam et al. 2024). Other studies suggest that China is responsible for anywhere from 20 to 50% of the gap (IISD 2024).

These findings on rising HFC emissions raise concerns about Chinese enforcement and monitoring.[6] Within formal diplomatic settings, contention over blame and respect has emerged amidst extraordinarily technical discussions concerning the HFC-23 emissions gap. In response to a US-submitted proposal that noted "with concern that emissions estimates derived for eastern China indicate emissions substantially higher than expected on the basis of reporting," China opined that the US proposal was "unscientific," "impractical," "disrespectful," and "framed a global issue as the problem of one party" (IISD 2024).[7]

* * * * *

In summary, China's engagement with the Montreal Protocol presents a mixed picture for China's environmental reputation. Official narratives describe

---

[6] Researchers suspect that other countries with high levels of HCFC-22 production, like India and Russia, are also contributing to the global emissions problem; however, atmospheric monitoring data was not available in those regions (Adam et al. 2024). See also EIA UK 2024.

[7] The US proposal also "request[ed] relevant parties to undertake requisite actions to implement HFC-23 emissions obligations and investigate the potential reasons for deviations between their reported emissions and emissions estimates derived from atmospheric monitoring" (IISD 2024).

China's involvement in moral and performance terms. China "attach[es] great importance to and conscientiously implement[s]" the Protocol (Zeng 2018). China's ratification of the Kigali amendment was characterized as Xi's "solemn pledge" to contribute to global environmental governance. China's substantive performance "account[ed] for more than half of the total amount [of ODS] eliminated by developing countries" (PRC MFA 2021). Apart from these self-serving statements, the evidence suggests that China has performed respectably in Montreal Protocol implementation and in diplomacy around the Kigali Amendment. On the other hand, China's enforcement problems with CFCs and HFC-23s raise lingering global concerns about China's ability to fulfill its environmental pledges.

3.2 UN Framework Convention on Climate Change

We now move from the narrower terrain of the Montreal Protocol to the vast expanse of climate change governance. In the area of climate change diplomacy, we see most clearly how China has moved from a defensive crouch toward the affirmative use of environmentalism to promote its strategic aims of building economic strength, improving foreign relations, and bolstering its reputation at home and abroad. In the Xi era, China has increasingly emphasized green development and ecological civilization as core aspects of its arrival on the global stage; and the strategic aspects of this effort can be clearly seen in Chinese climate diplomacy.

The 1992 UNFCCC established a global framework to "achieve ... stabilization of greenhouse gas concentrations in the atmosphere at a level that would prevent dangerous anthropogenic interference with the climate system" (UNFCCC, Art. 2). While the UNFCCC urges a "precautionary" approach under which a "lack of full scientific uncertainty" should not be used as a reason for postponing climate change measures, the treaty also evinces a deep concern with avoiding limits on economic development and supporting the idea of "common but differentiated responsibilities and respective capabilities" that puts the onus on developed countries to "take the lead in combating climate change and the adverse effects thereof" (UNFCCC, Art. 3). Under the 1997 Kyoto Protocol, developed countries were subject to binding emission reduction targets and more stringent reporting requirements, while China and some 128 other developing countries were not.

In the early 2000s, China benefitted from the absence of emissions reduction obligations under the Kyoto Protocol and was the largest beneficiary of funds transfers from developed countries under the Clean Development Mechanism. But China faced increasing pressure to reduce its GHG emissions, particularly after it surpassed the US in 2006 to become the world's largest emitter. Domestically, Chinese leaders were beginning to take the risks of climate change more seriously and coming to see environmental governance as a useful multipurpose tool for achieving economic development, energy security, social stability, environmental, and other goals.

In 2007, China released its first National Climate Change Program a few months before the UN climate conference in Bali. This program was hardly a custom-built program for climate action. It cobbled together myriad policies created for other reasons, including the one-child policy, deforestation policies aimed at preventing erosion and flooding, and long-term energy efficiency policies dating back to the 1980s.

In September 2009, President Hu Jintao, at the UN General Assembly, announced China's first ever carbon target, to reduce the amount of carbon emitted per unit of economic production by a "notable margin" (40–45% from 2005 levels by 2020). He also reiterated goals to increase the share of nonfossil fuels in China's primary energy consumption to "around 15%" by 2020; and to increase forest coverage and forest stock volume. At the same time, the speech reiterated China's long-established principles of CBDR, including "the imperative to give full consideration to the development stage and basic needs of developing countries," and the responsibility of developed countries to provide financing and technology to the developing world. Even as China hewed to its traditional, more defensive positions, it was bringing to the international stage commitments enabled by evolving domestic environmental and energy governance reforms.

At the Copenhagen conference in December 2009, international scrutiny on China was intense, seemingly catching Chinese negotiators off-guard. The US aggressively sought to break down the bifurcated Kyoto Protocol structure and attempted to limit international funding to China for climate action. China persisted in a largely defensive strategy. This included repeated invocation of CBDR and moral appeals to emissions justice, including China's relatively lower per capita and historical emissions and the contribution of developed country consumption to Chinese emissions (Conrad 2012; personal observations). Chinese interlocutors were combative. Chinese Vice Foreign Minister He Yafei said of the US climate negotiator "I think he lacks common sense when he made such a comment vis-a-vis China. He either lacks common sense or is extremely irresponsible." China's lone official side event, led by senior state think tank researcher Pan Jiahua, presented technical research arguing that the US and EU had already exceeded their fair share of carbon space and should pay China and the developing world to reduce emissions (personal observations). China formed a negotiating bloc of large, emerging economies with the so-called BASIC countries (Brazil, South Africa, India, and China) to resist binding emissions reduction targets for developing countries. Chinese representatives expressed satisfaction that the line between developed and developing countries had been maintained (Watts 2009), even as China was roundly criticized in the Western media as a blocker of a deal in Copenhagen (Lynas 2009).

China's public communications after Copenhagen were largely ineffective in countering this view. One of its first official communications post-Copenhagen, released on Christmas Day 2009, was a turgidly written article entitled "Verdant Mountains Cannot Stop Water Flowing; Eastward the River Keeps on Going – Premier Wen Jiabao at the Copenhagen Climate Change Conference" that mostly seemed designed to shield Wen from any accusations that he had caused the Copenhagen debacle (Zhao, et al. 2009). A year later at 2010 climate meetings in Tianjin, statements from Chinese negotiators only perpetuated this global image of China as an intransigent player. NDRC's Su Wei, for example, said the US was a "preening pig" that only criticized China and took inadequate measures to mitigate its own emissions (Buckley 2010). China's aggressive and defensive diplomacy might have garnered some accolades among Global South countries, but it played poorly among Western audiences.

In the wake of Copenhagen, China seemed to change tack on its climate strategy. In subsequent years, China has devoted an extraordinary amount of energy and resources to climate strategy, policy reform, and public communications. In the Xi era, Chinese leaders have increasingly sought to present the country as a climate leader. Chinese climate action has served to reinforce broader Chinese foreign relations messaging emphasizing the "win-win" nature of China's rise and arrival on the global stage. These moves have at times been presented in altruistic and moral terms by Chinese officials and interlocutors, or in civilizational terms (e.g., Chinese climate policy based on a "sense of responsibility to build a community with a shared future for mankind"). But most prominently, public messaging has emphasized more affirmative climate diplomacy and strengthened South–South climate cooperation.

Section 3.2.1 assesses changes in Chinese climate diplomacy, in particular China's affirmative diplomacy efforts and its expansion of cooperation with Global South countries. Section 3.2.2 discusses China's efforts domestically to comply with international climate obligations as well as critiques of those efforts. Section 3.2.3 examines how understandings of China's climate action (or lack thereof) have affected discourses and policy responses in the US.

3.2.1 More Affirmative Diplomacy

The change in China's approach to climate diplomacy from Copenhagen in 2009 to Paris in 2015 and beyond has been dramatic and is well-noted in the literature. Recognizing the limits of a more defensive approach and identifying increased alignment between Chinese domestic priorities and global climate objectives, China shifted decisively toward a more affirmative approach to climate diplomacy in the runup to the 2015 Paris climate negotiations and after. The shift has also come as China's rapidly growing emissions and its rise to become the world's second-largest economy have made its earlier, more defensive positions increasingly untenable.

China was widely praised for working with the US to consummate the Paris Agreement, which established the global framework for climate cooperation in place today. Xi and Obama made a joint announcement a year before the Paris meetings in November 2014 with specific commitments that would eventually become part of Chinese and US Paris pledges (US White House 2014). There, China committed to peak emissions at an unspecified level and to increase the share of nonfossil energy to 20% by 2030. Just months before the Paris meetings, in September 2015, the two leaders issued another joint statement that laid out a vision for the Paris Agreement that would eventually come to pass (US White House 2015). A post-Paris joint statement announced both countries' intentions to sign the Paris Agreement and "express[ed] their commitment to work together and with others to promote the full implementation of the Paris Agreement to win the fight against the climate threat" (US White House 2016).

Chinese decisionmakers saw Copenhagen in significant part as a communications failure and in the years after plowed resources into telling China's climate story. After 2011, the China delegation began to organize a "China Pavilion" at each climate gathering with panels of Chinese and international experts and exhibitions. These have become increasingly elaborate over the years and are now full-blown "meetings within a meeting" in their own right. Yeh & Loizeaux (2024) refer to the China Pavilion as a "key space for the performance of the country's climate governance position." The official China Pavilion at the 2023 COP 28 in Dubai, for example, featured more than 145 hours of programming on two stages over nine days, covering such topics as mitigation, adaptation, technology and finance, renewable energy, and climate cooperation. Panels also highlighted the role of subnational jurisdictions (Guangdong, Jiangsu, Shenzhen, Shanghai, and Hong Kong), youth, digital technology, and enterprises. China hosted more than 100 side events at COP28 Dubai, as compared to only one official side event at the 2009 COP15 meeting in Copenhagen.

Post-Paris, China has continued to take a more proactive, assertive approach to climate diplomacy. During the first Trump administration, Chinese leaders enjoyed a clear field on climate diplomacy as the US federal government retreated and actively opposed global climate action. China continued to work with US partners at the subnational level during this time. Xi took the unusual step of meeting with California Governor Jerry Brown (a subnational leader) in June 2017 to establish the California-China Climate Institute (CCCI). US-China climate cooperation resumed with the election of Joe Biden. In November 2021, the US and China released a joint declaration at COP26 in Glasgow on enhancing climate cooperation in the 2020s. In November 2023, Xie Zhenhua and John Kerry met in California to consummate the Sunnylands Statement on Enhancing Cooperation to Address the Climate Crisis. The US and China subsequently convened a global forum on methane emissions at COP28 in Dubai. Renewed climate cooperation was not immune from the impact of increased geopolitical tensions. Nancy Pelosi's August 2022 visit to Taiwan led China to temporarily suspend climate cooperation until late 2023. But China's willingness to revive climate cooperation is an indication of the benefits it sees in continued climate diplomacy. At the beginning of the second Trump administration, China is again positioning itself as a steady climate leader in the face of US antipathy toward climate action (Harvey 2025). China has not limited itself to cooperation with the US. It has continued cooperation with the EU, ASEAN, African states, and BRICS partner nations. In the 2023 leadup to COP28, China issued joint statements on climate cooperation with France and Brazil.

If China was unprepared at Copenhagen, a little more than a decade later it had built a climate diplomacy juggernaut – with substantial strategic and technical capacity and a willingness to steer the global climate agenda and make China's voice heard. China's strategy to present a more constructive face at climate negotiations has paid dividends in the public discourse. Whereas China was described as having "wrecked" the Copenhagen negotiations in 2009 (Lynas 2009), it garnered substantial accolades for its work to help bring to completion the Paris Agreement and in subsequent negotiations.

From the perspective of international norms, China has continued to rely on principles of sovereignty and CBDR to fend off unwanted legal obligations and to align itself with developing country interests. The US and others have long insisted that China should no longer be considered a developing country, given the size of its economy and the scale of its emissions. Yeh & Loizeaux (2024) show that China's approach can achieve results for developing countries as a whole – such as in maintenance of CBDR principles in the Paris Agreement or the agreement to create a Loss & Damage fund at the COP27 in 2022 – but it can also marginalize the interests of least powerful countries within developing country negotiating blocs, such as the Small Island Developing States and Least Developed Countries, and obscure injustices to subgroups of people within countries, such as displacement of Tibetan herders in an ecological restoration project listed within China's 2035 national adaptation plan.

China has also expanded its cooperation with Global South countries – what it calls "South–South" climate cooperation (Qi & Dauvergne 2022). South–South cooperation signals a shift from China as a recipient of support to a provider of assistance to developing countries. As of November 2024, China had signed fifty-three memoranda of understanding on South–South climate cooperation with 42 developing nations, trained some 10,000 people from over 120 countries on climate change action, and engaged in a variety of other research, training, and development aid cooperation (Hou 2024). As will be discussed next in Section 5, the expansion of South–South climate cooperation comes on the heels of decades of Chinese state-to-state collaboration with the US, the EU and individual European countries, Canada, Australia, and Japan.

Although China has no legal obligation under the UNFCCC to do so, it is increasingly providing climate finance to Global South countries under the umbrella of South–South climate cooperation.[8] In 2015, China pledged US $3.1 billion for a South–South Climate Cooperation Fund, although outside analysts say China has only provided a fraction of that amount as of 2023 (Tsang et al. 2023). Xie Zhenhua described China's position as follows: "China, the world's largest developing nation, will not compete with small island states, least-developed countries and African nations for the financial support ... but will instead offer other developing nations funding and technology via South–South climate cooperation" (Hou 2023). Developed and developing countries have pushed for countries with high emissions and high gross national income per capita like China to contribute to the funding base (PTI 2024; Greenfield & Harvey 2024). Chinese representatives insist that such contributions are voluntary and have resisted such efforts to alter existing norms (Hou 2024).

3.2.2 Domestic Climate Action: Accomplishments & Critiques

At Copenhagen, China could only bring to the table the beginnings of a comprehensive climate strategy. The country's first national climate policy in 2007 was largely an assembly of policies previously created for other

---

[8] Under Art. 9 of the Paris Agreement, developed countries "shall provide financial resources to assist developing countries with respect to both mitigation and adaptation" and "[o]ther Parties are encouraged to provide or continue to provide such support voluntarily."

purposes. Over the subsequent nearly twenty years, China has developed a comprehensive purpose-built climate change governance framework that Chinese state and society actors have begun to present as a model for other nations, particularly those in the Global South.

The October 2023 edition of *China's Policies and Actions for Addressing Climate Change* (PRC MEE 2023), an official report issued by China's environmental ministry, describes a substantial climate governance program and highlights successful Chinese performance against the key metrics listed in China's Nationally Determined Contributions (NDC) submission under the Paris Agreement (PRC 2022; see Table 3).

The document further spells out Chinese policies and actions to mitigate GHG emissions, adapt to climate change, further develop the national carbon emissions trading market, and develop "policy systems and supportive measures" for climate action such as legislation, policies, and standards; economic policies; statistical, accounting, and monitoring systems; and low-carbon city pilot projects.

The targets in the NDC – including interim 2025 targets – are implemented through what officials call a "1+N" framework. The "1" refers to two key central-level documents: *Guidelines for Comprehensive Implementation of the New Development Philosophy and the Achievement of Carbon Peak and*

Table 3 China NDC targets and progress

Target	2022 Progress
CO2 emissions peak before 2030	General progress
Carbon neutrality before 2060	General progress
Lower CO2 emissions per unit of GDP by 65% from 2005 levels by 2030	51%
Share of nonfossil energy in primary energy consumption to 25% by 2030	17.5%; total installed capacity of renewable energy 1.213 billion kW
Increase forest stock volume by 6 billion cubic meters from 2005 levels by 2030	Forest coverage rate at 24.02 percent (2021); forest stock of 19.493 billion m^3
Total installed capacity of wind & solar to 1.2 billion kW by 2030	365 million kW wind; 393 million kW solar (and 41 million kW biomass; 368 million kW hydropower; 55 million kW nuclear)

Neutrality Work, and the *Carbon Peaking Action Plan Before 2030*. The "N" refers to sector-specific and industry-specific plans and complementary measures. The plans cover the key sectors for climate mitigation: energy, industry, transportation, construction, agriculture, recycling, carbon sinks, and others. The key industries covered include coal, oil, natural gas, steel, building materials, nonferrous metals, petrochemicals, and new infrastructure (5G, data centers, Internet infrastructure, and the like). The N also includes regional and provincial plans for achieving local carbon targets. Chinese state-owned enterprises are required (and private firms are encouraged) to develop their own carbon peaking action plans.

In addition, China has in a relatively short span of time developed world-leading clean energy and electric transportation manufacturing and deployment. In 2022, China accounted for 55% of global investment in renewable energy at nearly half a trillion US dollars (Schonhardt 2023). It has become the leading investor in wind turbines, solar PV, hydropower, biomass energy, electric vehicles, charging infrastructure, energy efficient air conditioning and refrigeration, and a host of other technologies. Chinese manufacturing innovation and industrial policy have also contributed to dramatic cost declines. The levelized cost of energy from utility-scale solar, onshore and offshore wind fell by 58–74% from 2013 to 2023 (IEA 2022). The price of a lithium-ion battery pack has fallen by 88%. Trade related to Chinese demand for the raw materials of the clean energy transition, such as copper, lithium, cobalt, and nickel, have also become an important source of income in some countries. These China-led advances have transformed global possibilities for a clean energy transition.

Clean energy industries are now a major new source of economic growth that allow China to strengthen relationships with other countries through trade, investment, and supply of clean technologies while also making a contribution to achievement of global climate change and sustainable development goals. (Section 4 discusses these issues in greater detail in the context of China's green economic statecraft.)

Despite these signs of progress, China's climate actions remain contentious globally. For all who see China as a climate leader, there are equally vocal critics who consider China a climate laggard or a political threat. I discuss three areas of criticism: absolute emissions, China's coal revival, and human rights.

Absolute Emissions. That China could be considered a climate leader at all might seem odd. China's emissions more than tripled since China's entry into the WTO in 2001 to nearly 12 billion tons in 2022 – by far the largest emissions of any country and accounting for nearly 30% of global emissions. In 2021, China's emissions exceeded those in the US (11%), EU (7%), and India (7%) combined. The sheer volume of China's annual emissions makes it difficult to think of China as a leader on climate action. Indeed, Climate Action Tracker has called China's current climate targets, even if achieved, "highly insufficient" and "higher than what would be deemed 1.5 degrees C compatible."[9]

China has long countered this critique with arguments about emissions justice – noting China's lower historic and per capita emissions and the substantial portion of Chinese emissions produced for developed country consumption. China's economic rise, however, has rapidly altered these dynamics, such that Chinese per capita emissions now exceed per capita emissions in Europe. As of 2023, China passed the EU to become the second-largest historical emitter of GHGs, after only the US (Carbon Brief 2024). Also, with rising consumption of its own, the percentage of Chinese emissions associated with export has declined and China is now increasingly exporting emissions to other countries, replicating historic patterns of pollution export from the US and Europe to China.

Continued Reliance on Coal. China's continued reliance on coal has been another source of vociferous global criticism. In 2023, China accounted for more than 50% of global consumption. In contrast to the full-throated support Chinese leaders have given to carbon peaking and neutrality targets, their public statements on coal have urged caution. Xi Jinping has spoken of a "build it before you break it" strategy (*xianli houpo*) – widely understood to be an admonition to move away from coal judiciously and only after firmly establishing a new system based on clean energy. This policy appeared to be motivated by concerns about energy security, national self-reliance, and the possibility of overzealous local bureaucratic compliance with new low-carbon targets.

Critics have been concerned that the policy represents Chinese backtracking on decarbonization or will allow local actors to undermine Chinese climate action. Outside observers have looked on in dismay as Chinese coal mines have reopened and permitting of coal plants has continued at a blistering pace. In 2022, Chinese regulators permitted "[a] total of 106 GW of new coal power projects . . ., the equivalent of two large coal power plants per week" (Myllyvirta 2023). These plants have generally been designated as "supporting generation sources," because national policy as of February 2022 prohibits approval of new coal-fired power plants for bulk power generation. Chinese interlocutors have said that new coal plants will not operate at significant hours since they are being built as back-up power to support grid stability and intermittent renewables, but it remains to be seen whether this will be the case in practice (Myllyvirta 2023, p. 14).

---

[9] The US and EU are each rated by Climate Action Tracker as merely "insufficient."

Chinese overseas construction of coal plants has been another major point of contention. For a time, China's role as the "world's largest exporter of coal-fired power plant finance and technology" was considered by many a key reason China could not be considered a climate leader. Xi Jinping's September 2021 announcement that China would no longer build new coal-fired power plants abroad has shifted attention to whether that pledge is being implemented. The issue of China's overseas coal investments is discussed further in Section 4.

Human Rights. Human rights issues have also become part of discussions about climate change in at least two different ways. Most prominently, China has been accused of human rights violations related to its climate actions. Chinese firms have allegedly used forced Uyghur labor in solar PV manufacturing, benefitted from child labor in artisanal cobalt mining in the Congo, and enabled land grabs and poor labor conditions in Indonesian nickel mining (CECC 2023b; CRI 2024). Human rights groups have accused China of using "environmental policy as a tool of state control" (Wang 2022). In response, Chinese officials and companies have generally denied these allegations or refused comment. Human rights concerns have been a major cause of negative public opinion toward China in developed countries (Silver 2022a).

Moreover, Chinese limits on environmental civil society groups, lawyers, and media create a complicated environment for the implementation of climate policies and governance and threaten to constrain global access to information about Chinese climate action (Wang 2018a). Environmental groups navigate complex political and legal dynamics to find space for advocacy (Gao & Teets 2020). Lawyers and environmental lawsuits can face substantial barriers to litigating over the environment (Wang 2011). Environmental journalists face censorship in reporting on pollution and climate change. A key concern is that both weak and overzealous implementation will not come to light absent a more open system of participation and accountability.

3.2.3 China and Climate in the US Political Context

The debates referenced previously are part of the contestation over how to think about China's climate actions (or lack thereof). Chinese progress on climate diplomacy, governance, and clean technology production butt up against serious concerns about the scale and trajectory of China's emissions, economic and security risks, and the illiberal aspects of Chinese governance. These play into the sense of China as a climate leader or laggard. Friend or enemy. Hero or zero.

These conflicts appear in policy debates over climate change and China in other countries, including the US. The US Senate's 1997 Byrd-Hagel Resolution, approved by a 95-0 vote, stated the "sense of the Senate" that the

US should not join any protocol to the UNFCCC that did not impose emissions reductions mandates on developing countries like China and India. China has even emerged amidst arguments about the legal standing of US state plaintiffs to sue in the US Supreme Court case *Massachusetts v. EPA* (2007).[10] More recently, Senate Majority Leader Mitch McConnell said in 2014 of China's goal to peak carbon emissions that it "requires the Chinese to do nothing at all for 16 years."

US concerns about Chinese human rights abuses and economic and security risks from Chinese clean energy advances have also spurred policy responses (US White House 2018; UESRC 2022; CECC 2023a). The US Uyghur Forced Labor Prevention Act (2021), for example, bans certain goods produced in Xinjiang from import into the US absent "clear and convincing evidence" they were not produced through forced labor. In February 2024, the Biden administration announced an investigation into "connected automobiles with technology from countries of concern" to address national security risks, "part of a broader effort to stop E.V. and other smart-car imports from China" (US White House 2024).

The US has also passed measures aimed at protecting US jobs and companies from perceived unfair Chinese trade practices. These actions have also been justified in terms of supply chain resilience and diversification to avoid supply chain bottlenecks that emerged during COVID. The US Inflation Reduction Act established local content restrictions that do not allow subsidies if the vehicle's battery or battery components are manufactured or assembled by a "foreign entity of concern" affiliated with China, Russia, Iran, or North Korea. US tariffs on Chinese-made solar products have been justified on economic and national security grounds. These tariffs were initially imposed against Chinese solar manufacturers under antidumping and countervailing duty laws in 2012 during the Obama administration and were later expanded or extended under various legal authorities by the Trump and Biden administrations. Whether these reflect good policy and appropriate assessment of risk or not is a subject of intense debate. What is undeniable is that the perception of China as an enemy and not a friend is being used to justify an ever-growing set of policies to contain China.

In certain instances, China is playing the useful role of bogeyman for industry advocates and politicians opposed to any US climate change action at all.

---

[10] "EPA overstates its case in arguing that its decision not to regulate contributes so insignificantly to petitioners' injuries that it cannot be haled into federal court, and that there is no realistic possibility that the relief sought would mitigate global climate change and remedy petitioners' injuries, especially since predicted increases in emissions from China, India, and other developing nations will likely offset any marginal domestic decrease EPA regulation could bring about." (USSC 2007, at 3).

Industry's role in opposing climate regulation and spreading misinformation about climate change is well documented. One can see how the corporate interests of the fossil fuel industry are aligned with arguments that portray China as a bad actor on climate change (Green-Weiskel 2022). However, even among supporters of climate action, China figures into arguments about the fair allocation of burdens and responsibilities. US National Security Advisor Jake Sullivan, for example, has said that China should not "hide behind any kind of claim that they are a developing nation" in order to slow-roll efforts to cut emissions.

* * * * *

The dynamics we see in the context of Chinese engagement with the Montreal Protocol and the UNFCCC appear elsewhere as well. In the global biodiversity context, China has become a more proactive player with regard to the UN Convention on Biological Diversity (CBD) (Qin 2020). Most prominently, China hosted the COVID-interrupted COP15 of the CBD, which was eventually bifurcated between a mostly virtual session from Kunming in October 2021 and a second meeting held in Montreal in December 2022. Chinese leaders seemed to view COP15 as an opportunity to further assert a role as a global leader, even bringing key Chinese political slogans like ecological civilization squarely into the international treaty context (Chinese authorities chose "Ecological Civilization: Building a Shared Future for All Life on Earth" as the official conference slogan) (Lu & Harlan 2021; Rodenbiker 2023b). These meetings resulted in the Kunming-Montreal Global Biodiversity Framework (GBF), an important achievement, and allowed China to put on display the fruits of a burgeoning domestic environmental governance framework for biodiversity, including development of a broader system of protected areas and national parks, a national "ecological conservation red line" policy (essentially a land-use planning system for ecologically important areas), and others (PRC SCIO 2021b; Wang-Kaeding 2021, p. 31).

China is having some success in promoting its environmental actions on the global stage. It has been more assertive in diplomatic contexts, including the Montreal Protocol, the UNFCCC, and the CBD, and has aggressively expanded its public communications capacity, particularly in the years after the Copenhagen climate conference. This has introduced Chinese viewpoints into information environments previously dominated by the US and Europe. Chinese diplomatic positions are also enabled by substantial climate-related reforms at the domestic level. Yet, persistent global concerns about the sheer scale of Chinese environmental impacts, weaknesses in implementation, and the illiberal aspects to China's approach to governance continue to weaken trust and draw combative responses from other countries.

4 Green Economic Statecraft

This section turns to a discussion of China's green economic statecraft. Economic statecraft is the use of economic actions to achieve foreign policy and national security goals, and green economic statecraft focuses on mobilization of green development for such purposes.

China formally launched its Going Out policy in 2000 to obtain resources, seek new markets, and upgrade the competitiveness of Chinese companies. Xi Jinping's launch of the Belt and Road Initiative (BRI) in 2013 accelerated Chinese outbound investment and trade and drew greater international scrutiny of the statecraft aspects of China's global economic activities. This scrutiny has included accusations of debt-trap diplomacy, concerns about improper Chinese political influence, and criticisms over lack of transparency and uneven benefits within partner countries. Environmental concerns have emerged as a leading component of the global China critique.

Green economic statecraft first emerged as a way to dampen the environmental risks associated with economic activity, but it is evolving into a strategy that takes advantage of China's emergence as the global leader in the manufacturing and deployment of clean technologies. This means higher value-added economic opportunities for China, new markets to absorb Chinese domestic overcapacity, and growing leverage to promote geopolitical and foreign policy objectives. Green economic statecraft, in other words, allows China to exert power in a number of ways – by building Chinese economic strength, increasing other countries' reliance on China through trade and investment, and bolstering China's reputation through contributions to global environmental and sustainable development goals.

The first two case studies in this section – on fossil energy investment and clean energy development – show how Chinese economic statecraft serves to counter criticisms of China and achieve a range of economic, political, and environmental goals. The third case study, a place-based study on Chinese green development in Chile, illustrates one country's "pragmatic" response to Chinese green development. In Chile, the interplay of local economic and environmental interests, relatively strong institutions, and historic dynamics with developed countries have generated a receptivity to engagement with China and skepticism of US and Europe warnings about China.

4.1 Fossil Energy Investment

Chinese overseas financing of fossil fuel energy projects has been a focal point for criticism of global China. More than 70% of the US $225 billion that Chinese overseas public development finance institutions – China

Development Bank (CDB) and China Export-Import Bank (China Ex-Im Bank) – invested in energy projects from 2000 to 2017 was in fossil fuel projects (Kong 2019, p. 17). This includes oil (41%), coal (20%), and gas (13%) projects. Of nonfossil projects, hydropower projects account for 18%, with the remainder (less than 10%) to nuclear, solar, wind, and geothermal projects.

These investments increased rapidly in the years after the 2008 global financial crisis. Geographically, the projects had relatively even regional distribution with 28% each to Asia, Europe, and Latin American and 15% to Africa (Kong 2019). The investments have been mostly in power generation (45%); exploration and extraction (36%); and transmission and distribution (10%) (Kong 2019). During this period, China became the leader in overseas development finance for energy projects, passing other major financiers like the US, Japan, France, and South Korea. Between 2007 and 2014, Chinese overseas development finance for energy exceeded the combined amount of finance from Western-backed multilateral development banks, such as the World Bank, ADB, the Inter-American Development Bank, and the African Development Bank.

Chinese overseas investments in coal-fired power plants have drawn the most vociferous criticism as incompatible with Paris Agreement goals. From 2006 to 2021, China was the world's largest public financier of overseas coal-fired power plants with about 54 GW of coal power projects in twenty countries (Kong & Gallagher 2021). The US government, the World Bank, and other institutions began to restrict financing for coal projects in 2013. After this exit from coal, China, Japan, and Korea were the only major public financiers of coal projects until 2020–21 (Wang et al. 2024).

The academic literature has highlighted three primary drivers of Chinese overseas investment in coal projects: Chinese industrial policy, host country demand, and Chinese company initiative (Kong 2019; Davidson et al. 2023, Nedopil 2023; Wang et al. 2024). Kong, for example, argues that Chinese industrial policy support for overseas energy projects is motivated by several needs: the search for new markets to absorb Chinese domestic overcapacity and to acquire advanced technologies, the need to manage foreign exchange risk, and demand for natural resources.

In September 2021, Xi Jinping announced at the UN General Assembly that China would "step up support for other developing countries in developing green and low-carbon energy and will not build new coal-fired power projects abroad" (Xinhua 2021). This announcement came a year after Japan and South Korea made similar announcements to restrict public finance of coal projects in 2020. China received plaudits for this move from many, although others expressed concern about whether the policy would be implemented effectively.

A complex mix of factors contributed to China shifting away from carbon intensive overseas investments. Davidson et al. (2023) argue that China, Japan, and South Korea restricted public financing for coal projects in 2020 and 2021 because of reduced host country demand and international pressure to cease coal financing, which in turn weakened domestic Chinese coal interests opposed to an overseas coal ban. Since 2015, twenty-seven developing countries cancelled coal power projects amounting to 77% of the preconstruction pipeline in those countries. Scholars have also begun to unpack variation in host country demand through detailed ground-level studies. Liu et al. (2022) explain that Pakistan was more receptive to Chinese renewable energy investment because it had no domestic source of coal, and the construction of coal-fired power plants would only exacerbate energy security risk. In other countries, Chinese coal projects encountered active opposition and legal obstruction in several countries with resultant reputational harm for China. The Lamu coal power project – financed and developed by Chinese institutions – was halted by Kenyan courts after an environmental group (deCoalinize) sued, arguing that the government had not completed a proper environmental impact assessment (BBC 2019).

Nedopil (2023) likewise emphasizes increased economic, social, and political risks to explain Chinese willingness to retreat from overseas investment in coal. In addition to reduced host country demand for coal projects and local and global political opposition, the financial risks of coal projects have increased, including increased sovereign debt risk in recipient countries, higher financing costs as global investors exited from coal finance, greater coal price volatility, and rising average coal prices. After 2017, project developers and development banks alike became more cautious about coal power plants due to changed economics and increased disruptions related to environmental and social risks. China has been promoting the idea of "small yet beautiful projects" (*xiao er mei*) globally and this has been reflected in practice in lower average deal sizes in the last few years (Nedopil 2025).

To summarize, lower host country demand, rising international and domestic pressure, and shifting economics for Chinese companies weakened the pull and push for such projects. Furthermore, the availability of a green alternative (and the participation of major Chinese companies in these alternatives) and the reputational gains of an overseas coal exit helped to weaken the China-side push. The revival of coal plant permitting and coal mining within China under the mantra of energy security and economic recovery post-COVID also relieved some of the overcapacity problem that would otherwise have been dealt with through overseas projects.

Have China's pledges been implemented in practice? No new coal plants with Chinese participation have been announced since 2021 (Nedopil 2025). Nedopil

(2025) further notes that China's 2024 overseas energy engagement was the "greenest since the BRI's inception in 2013." This included record investment in green energy (solar, wind, and biomass) and hydropower. At the same time, some coal power projects commenced before 2021 – such as Bangladesh's Barisal 2 and Gacko II in Bosnia – continued after the 2021 announcement, and China has continued overseas investment in other types of fossil fuel projects (e.g., gas, oil, and coal mining).

4.2 Clean Energy Technologies

Clean energy technologies are at the heart of China's new approach to green development. These refer most prominently to what are colloquially known as "the new three" (*xin san yang*) – solar power, EVs, and batteries. But they also include wind power, hydrogen electrolyzers, hydropower, energy efficiency, rail, grid, nuclear power and a host of other categories of goods and services. In 2023, investment and the value of goods and services in clean energy industries amounted to 9% of China's entire GDP and year-on-year growth in clean energy accounted for 40% of all GDP growth (Myllyvirta 2024).

The original motivations for state support of these industries were in significant part economic (Hilton 2024). They have been included in several waves of what Chen and Naughton (2016) have called "techno-industrial policy." After a period of increased marketization and the retreat of the state during the 1980s and 90s, China began a long-term embrace of industrial policy after 2003 that continues to this day. In contrast to industrial policy in Japan and Korea, which was oriented toward technological "catch up," Chinese techno-industrial policy has been aimed at leap-frogging existing technologies to seek growth in industries without dominant global incumbents. As previously mentioned, motivations for industrial policy support of clean technologies in particular include energy security, mitigation of environmental limits to development, pollution reduction, social unrest, and international pressures for China to address climate change (Boyd 2012; personal observations).

Importantly, China's push to develop clean technology industries was also motivated by a "conviction that China has an historic opportunity to position itself as an economic and technological leader in a global transition towards low-carbon energy" (Boyd 2012). Boyd (2012) discusses the writings of Hu Angang, a well-known professor at Tsinghua University, in this regard as indicative of the motivations behind China's support for clean technologies:

> [Hu] notes that different waves of industrialisation and modernisation have been tied to the emergence of important new energy technologies. Historically, the countries that have been able to effectively exploit these

new energy technologies before anyone else have succeeded in increasing their influence and changing the balance of power in the international system [citations omitted]. Hu argues that China has consistently failed to position itself at the forefront of these crucial technological breakthroughs, and as a result, has remained politically marginalised for much of its modern history. China must not "make the same mistakes once again," but must rather "have a strong sense of crisis" in order to become an economic and political leader in the 'next wave' of modernisation, which will be defined by low-carbon energy technologies [citations omitted].

The state push for renewable energy included the passage of China's Renewable Energy Law (2005) and the elevation of renewable energy to a national priority in the Mid- to Long-term Development Plan for Renewable Energy (2007). Solar, wind, and electric vehicles were listed as favored industries within China's 2010 Strategic Emerging Industries policy and the 2015 Made in China 2025 strategy. Sectoral plans in China's 13th and 14th five-year plans (2016–25) included targets for renewable energy and new energy vehicles. Batteries received support for research and development from MOST's 863 program, and Chinese EV manufacturers benefitted from a host of subsidies and policies promoting technology transfer and access to critical raw materials that set the stage for China's later global dominance in battery and EV supply chains (Graham 2021).

Clean Energy Manufacturing. This sustained policy and fiscal support have helped Chinese companies to achieve global dominance in key clean energy technologies. For example:

- *Solar.* China's global share of silica-based solar PV modules manufacturing was more than 70% in 2021. Share of the production of the cells that compose these modules was more than 80%, and the share of wafers used to manufacture cells was more than 90% (IEA 2023).
- *Wind.* Chinese companies account for more than 55% of global wind turbine manufacturing capacity in 2021 (He et al. 2022).
- *EVs and Batteries.* China dominates at every stage of the EV and battery supply chain, accounting for more than 60% share of EV manufacturing capacity, three-quarters of global battery cell production, nearly 80% of cathode production, and more than 90% of anode production (IEA 2024a, p. 30). It also dominates in the material processing of critical minerals like graphite (nearly 100%), cobalt (about 75%), and lithium (more than 60%). Critical minerals mining is more geographically diverse, but Chinese companies are active in all the key jurisdictions, including Australia and Chile (lithium), Indonesia (nickel), and the Democratic Republic of Congo (cobalt).

Clean Energy Deployment. China has also been a global leader in domestic deployment of clean energy technologies, driven by fiscal and policy support aimed at meeting the industrial policy, energy security, geopolitical, and reputational objectives discussed earlier.

- *Solar.* As of 2024, China had a world-leading 660 GW of installed solar capacity. In 2023 alone, China added 216.9 GW, more than the entire solar installed capacity in the second-place country, the US.
- *Wind.* China is the global leader in installed onshore and offshore wind capacity as well. It had 475 GW of onshore wind at the end of 2023, nearly triple the amount of wind power installed in the US. Offshore wind installations reached 31.5 GW with the UK in second place at 14.5 GW. The US accounts for less than 1% of global offshore wind deployment as of this writing.
- *Electric vehicles.* Slightly more than half of EVs (BEV and PHEV) globally were registered in China as of 2023, compared to 28% in Europe, only 12% in the US, and a mere 6% in the rest of the world (IEA 2024b).

Perhaps more than any other aspect of Chinese global environmentalism, China's progress on clean energy technologies has garnered China accolades among global and domestic audiences. These technologies are essential for the achievement of global climate targets, such as the goal to triple global renewable energy capacity by 2030 agreed to at COP28 in Dubai. Chinese manufacture and deployment of these technologies has dramatically lowered costs. This in turn has allowed for global deployment to far exceed projections and increases the likelihood of successful clean energy transitions in developed and developing countries alike.

Yet Chinese dominance has raised strategic concerns in the US and Europe and an aggressive policy response. Current debates in the US and other developed countries have raised a diverse range of reasons to oppose Chinese clean technology dominance, including concerns about unfair trade practices, prevention of espionage, supply chain resilience, human rights, protection of developed country jobs and their pillar industries like the auto industry, and realist concerns about maintaining a substantial enough edge over China in power.

The Biden administration implemented a broad policy response to this Chinese dominance in clean energy technologies. In May 2024, the administration announced a 100% tariff on Chinese-made EVs, 25% tariffs on EV batteries from China and certain critical minerals, and an increase in Chinese solar panel tariffs to 50%. To compete with Chinese industrial policy, Congress also passed three pieces of legislation – the Inflation Reduction Act, the Bipartisan Infrastructure Law, and the CHIPS and Science Act – that collectively set forth the contours of an American industrial policy in clean energy technologies, mobilizing hundreds of billions of dollars in support for renewable energy, EVs, and other technologies. Biden also signed into law the Uyghur Forced Labor Prevention Act in 2021, which created a rebuttable presumption that goods made in Xinjiang (such as solar raw materials and products) are made with forced labor. These measures came on top of solar tariffs the Trump administration imposed in 2018 and Obama-era solar tariffs imposed in 2012 and 2014–15. The US also brought and won a WTO trade case against China between 2012 and 2014 concerning Chinese export controls on rare earth metals, tungsten, and molybdenum. The EU has responded to Chinese dominance in clean energy technologies with measures of its own. These include tariffs on imported Chinese EVs and laws like the Net-Zero Industry Act and the Critical Raw Materials Act, which incentivize domestic EU clean energy technology production and aim to ensure secure and sustainable access to critical minerals.

These are the contours of the contestation over Chinese clean energy dominance. The competing narratives could not differ more starkly. Contrast, for example, the US Trade Representative's characterization of Chinese practices as predatory and unfair to more positive accounts in the literature arguing that China's clean energy dominance has come from sustained policy support, industry clusters, global links, and talent cultivation (Nahm 2021; Hove 2024; USTR 2024). It remains uncertain which narratives will prevail, but if China continues to be seen as an enemy to the US and Europe then policies to constrain and limit Chinese clean technologies will persist.

4.3 Chinese Green Development in Chile

Our final case of this section looks at Chinese green development in Chile as an example of contention over China occurring beyond the US and Europe. Chile has become a country of interest in the geopolitical competition between China and the US/Europe in significant part because it is a major source of copper and lithium – two critical minerals essential to the global clean energy transition. Chile is also a country with aggressive plans to decarbonize domestically. Chile has abundant renewable resources with national strategic plans to achieve carbon neutrality by 2050 and 80% of the energy mix from renewables by 2030 (WEF 2024). Chile also has announced plans to become a global leader in the export of green hydrogen (WEF 2024).

This snapshot of the Chilean situation reveals a few initial findings. *First*, China has offered important support for the Chilean economy through trade and investment. In recent years, this has been concentrated in areas related to green development. For Chilean goals of moving up the value chain, Chinese firms have also been more willing to strike deals, whereas US and European actors have not so far moved much beyond rhetoric. *Second*, American and European officials have sought to warn Chileans of the security risks associated with Chinese engagement, but this has not to date driven the same sort of hawkish response in Chile that we have seen in the US and to a lesser extent the EU. *Third*, although Chilean companies and politicians have been less receptive to security arguments, they express concern about excessive economic reliance on China and are actively seeking to diversify their economic engagements in the green development space.

Historically, Chile and China have what both sides have called a "special relationship" (Bartlett 2024). Under socialist president Salvador Allende, Chile was the first country in South America to establish diplomatic relations with the PRC on December 15, 1970. Chile continued ties with China after General Augusto Pinochet's 1973 coup d'état, despite the Pinochet regime's anti-Communist leanings and embrace of free market policies. Chilean copper exports to China underpinned (and still underpin) an emerging commercial trade relationship. Chile was the first Latin American country to support China's accession to the WTO in 2001, and it was the first individual nation to sign a free trade agreement with China in 2005. Trade between the two countries grew at a staggering pace – from US$8.1 billion in 2005 to $57.2 billion in 2023 with China becoming Chile's top trade partner after 2009, passing the US. As of 2022, China purchased nearly 40% of Chilean exports, including about 70% of copper exports. Chilean experts worry about excessive reliance on trade with China and hope for greater diversification among China, the US, Europe, and other Asian countries like Japan and Korea.

Chinese foreign direct investment in Chile was not an important part of the relationship until the 2010s. As of 2014, Chile became one of China's top ten destinations for FDI and after 2018 has been the leading country in Latin America and the Caribbean for Chinese investment, with major, USD multibillion-dollar investments in critical minerals and electricity generation, transmission, and distribution.

The first major Chinese investment in Chile came with State Power Investment Corporation's (SPIC) 2016 acquisition of Pacific Hydro from an Australian pension fund. SPIC is one of China's five largest power generation companies. Pacific Hydro held US $1 billion in largely hydropower assets in Chile at the time of acquisition and has since completed an 82 MW wind farm with further plans to develop major wind and solar farm projects. This was followed by Tianqi Lithium's purchase of a 24% stake in Chile's Sociedad Quimica y Minera (SQM), completed in 2018. Tianqi, a private Chinese company, and SQM were the third and fourth largest lithium companies in the world by production value in 2018 and major players in the supply chain for electric vehicle batteries.

Chinese companies have since completed several USD billion-dollar transactions involving Chilean electric grid assets as well. In 2018, China Southern Power Grid purchased a 27.7% stake in Transelec from Canada's Brookfield Infrastructure for US $1.3 billion. Transelec is Chile's main electricity transmission provider with power lines reaching 98% of the Chilean public. State Grid Corporation of China (SGCC) purchased Chilquinta Energia from US company Sempra Energy for US $2.23 billion in 2020 and 97% of CGE from Spain's Naturgy Energy Group for US $3.03 billion in 2021. These are two of Chile's four main electricity distribution companies, representing 57% of the country's distribution system. Chinese companies have further invested in other renewable energy projects (wind, solar, hydropower), train and commuter rail lines, salmon aquaculture, and fruit farms.

China is also beginning to play a role in Chile's move toward electrified transportation. Chile's 2021 National Electromobility Strategy sets nonbinding targets for 100% zero-emission vehicles for new sales of urban buses and light-duty and light commercial vehicles by 2035 and freight transport and intercity buses by 2045 (Chilean Govt. 2022; Delgado & Logiodice 2025). Chile has also announced plans to sell only EV passenger vehicles after 2035 and to achieve 40% passenger EV penetration by 2050 (Urrutia-Mosquera & Flórez-Calderón 2024). As of this writing, Santiago boasts the largest municipal electric bus fleet outside of China and has 2550 e-buses in operation with 4,406 expected by the end of 2025 (Sustainable Bus 2025). The fleet appears to be composed entirely of Chinese e-buses from Foton, BYD, Yutong, King Long, Zhongtong, and Higer (Sustainable Bus 2025).

This Chinese investment has raised some political concerns within Chile, although the deals have mostly been approved. Chinese company purchases of grid assets and the Tianqi Lithium acquisition have drawn the most scrutiny. These led to proposals (ultimately not approved) to establish a committee for security review of foreign investments or to allow Chile's congress to block investments of strategic assets by foreign SOEs (Fuentes 2020).

A closer look at the Tianqi Lithium acquisition is illustrative. Although copper remains Chile's most important export, lithium is a rapidly growing area central to electric vehicles production. Chile is the second largest producer of lithium (49,000 tons in 2024) after Australia (88,000 tons in 2024) with extraction operations run by SQM and US company Albemarle in Chile's northern Atacama Desert (USGS 2025, p. 111). Other major producers include China, Zimbabwe, Argentina, and Brazil. Tianqi's acquisition from Canadian fertilizer company, Nutrien, when proposed, faced an antitrust appeal from Chile's development agency Corfo, which expressed concern that the acquisition would "gravely distort market competition" (De la Jara 2018). Tianqi is also a 51% owner of the Greenbushes mine in Western Australia, the world's largest hard-rock lithium mine.

Although Tianqi itself has repeatedly emphasized that it is a private company, Chinese officials made clear that they would act on behalf of the company if necessary. In 2018, as Tianqi's proposed deal underwent antitrust review, China's ambassador to Chile Xu Bu threatened Chile, saying that it would "leave negative influences on the development of economic and commercial relations between both countries" if Chile did not approve the Tianqi transaction (Jamasmie 2018). Chilean authorities ultimately allowed the deal but imposed limits on Tianqi's board membership and its access to sensitive SQM business information.

Despite these concerns, Chileans seem to have viewed US warnings about China with some skepticism. Several interviewees I spoke to in Santiago suggested that US warnings were seen as hypocritical given past US interventions in Chilean politics. They contrasted US support for the overthrow of the Allende government with a positive, long-term trade relationship with China. They also commented on the negative optics of US Southern Command (Southcom) director Laura Richardson – the leading American military officer in the region – publicly warning of Chinese influence in Chile, while also working with US companies in the region to "box out" China on lithium (see, e.g., Atlantic Council 2023, at 45:00–46:00).

Contributing to Chile's openness to China is the fact that Chinese companies have been willing to take up Chilean invitations to help the country move up the EV value chain, whereas the US and Europe are seen as raising warnings about risk from China without taking actions that benefit Chile (interview with Chilean academic 2023). For example, the Boric administration in Chile has sought to tie access to lithium concessions to commitments to invest in lithium processing capacity within Chile. At present, China dominates lithium processing and much of Chile's raw lithium is shipped to China for further processing. In response to Chilean calls, two Chinese companies – BYD and Tsingshan – agreed to build lithium processing in Chile. In 2023, Tsingshan announced a plan to invest US $233 million in a lithium iron phosphate plant in Chile in exchange for preferential prices for lithium from SQM until 2030. Chilean President Boric said in relation to the Tsingshan announcement: "We are not going to limit ourselves only to the extraction of nonmetallic minerals, but we are also going to create value chains and also transfer knowledge because one of the commitments that the company has made is to generate exchange programmes for Chilean professionals to travel to China and also train in the development of this industry." Chinese company BYD announced a similar deal for a lithium cathode plant in northern Chile in 2023. In a major setback, though, Chile's Corfo announced the termination of both projects in May 2025, citing changing global market dynamics and declining lithium prices (Lu & Han 2025). A new Corfo tender seeking proposals for high-value-added lithium projects issued in April 2025 has had no takers as of this writing.

US and European actors have shown interest in working with Chile but have not yet announced new deals. Former US Ambassador to Chile, Bernadette Meehan, announced in 2024 that US companies have shown "intense interest" in expanding lithium extraction and production of lithium-based products (Canbero & Solomon 2024). German Chancellor Olaf Scholz suggested during a January 2023 trip to Chile that German companies would help Chile to move up the value chain and avoid Chinese exploitation, but no German companies have to date stepped forward to implement the pledge (Osborn 2023). Some in Chile have also noted the risk that the US Inflation Reduction Act may harm Chilean green development goals by pulling investment away from Chile to the US with its generous subsidies for green hydrogen and other clean investments (interview with Chilean official 2024).

Moreover, the US has played a role in blocking or creating difficulties for several high-profile China-related investments outside of the clean technology space. A proposed submarine fiber optic cable between Chile and China was canceled after warnings from then US Secretary of State Mike Pompeo in 2018. In 2021, Chile canceled a contract originally awarded to Chinese technology firm Aisino to produce Chilean identity cards and passports after US officials raised security concerns and threatened to revoke Chilean visa waiver status if the deal were to go through (MERICS 2022).

Chile is a quintessential example of what I have called a pragmatic response to China's rise. Chilean government and business elites see engagement with China as desirable in significant part because the economic opportunities of the relationship are too important to ignore. What's more, China's recent focus on green development promises to combine economic and environmental opportunities in a manner attractive to Chileans. The threat of Chinese inroads has also appeared to generate competition among other countries for Chilean favor. In 2022, for example, the US initiated the Americas Partnership for Economic Prosperity as a counter to Chinese investment in Latin America, although the effort was criticized for lacking investment resources (Hawkins 2023).

How are different segments of Chilean society responding to Chinese engagement with Chile? Here we have largely considered Chilean political and economic elites who make policy and consummate business deals.

Academics with a critical view of past US interventions in Chile have also been receptive to Chinese economic engagements with Chile (interviews with Chilean academics 2023, 2024). While many were cognizant of potential risks of economic dependency on China, they also offered that Chilean institutions were up to the task of mitigating potential problems. What of environmentalists? Local green groups I spoke with were taking a wait-and-see approach. They were aware of Western critiques of Chinese environmental impacts in Latin America, but were still learning about Chinese actions in Chile (interview with Chilean environmentalists 2023). The largest Chinese lithium investment in Chile was merely a financial stake in the Chilean lithium company, rather than extraction carried out by Chinese actors. Environmental concerns about the impact of lithium extraction on ecosystems and local flora and fauna like the pink flamingo are growing, but China has not been the focal point of criticisms here given the leading role of SQM and Albemarle. If Chinese companies follow through on pledges to build industrial facilities in Chile, critiques of the environmental impacts of Chinese projects may grow louder. These debates go beyond China and center on the economic and environmental tradeoffs presented by a low-carbon transition or economic development in general, but China will more likely become the target of critiques as its role grows.

5 Green Development Cooperation

On the west side of central Beijing at No. 5 Houyingfang Hutong, there is a building called the International Environmental Convention Compliance Building (*guoji huanjing gongyue lüyue dasha*). Within are the offices of the Ministry of Ecology & Environment's Foreign Environmental Cooperation Center (FECO) and a substantial concentration of China's major official environmental cooperation programs, old and new. These include the long-standing CCICED, founded in 1992 as a partnership among senior Chinese environmental leaders and international donors, and the more recent BRIGDC, a partnership between China's environmental ministry, environmental ministries from BRI countries, UN agencies, and nongovernmental green groups established in April 2019 after the second Belt and Road Forum for International Cooperation (Zhao & Hanson 2024). The offices of the Shanghai Cooperation Organization (SCO) Environmental Information Sharing Platform, the Lancang-Mekong Environmental Cooperation Center, the National Center for Climate Change Strategy and International Cooperation (NCSC), and the Global Center on Adaptation can also be found in the building. Here, governance institutions and physical infrastructure combine to signal Chinese commitments to green development and international cooperation. These institutions represent, however, only a portion of China's emerging green development cooperation – namely, the segment organized by China's environmental ministry and affiliates. Green development cooperation is also emerging elsewhere, initiated by other central and provincial government ministries, think tanks, research centers, state-owned and private enterprises, and civil society organizations (Harlan & Lu 2022, p. 479).

As an initial matter, we should define the scope of the term "green development cooperation." In this Element, we use the term to refer to various forms of "soft" technical cooperation and assistance, including joint research, capacity building, dialogues, and environmental projects.[11]

As with Chinese green diplomacy and economic statecraft, Chinese actors are becoming more active in the green development cooperation space. The efforts run by the Chinese government and affiliates as well as state-owned enterprises are naturally the most clearly aimed at conveying positive accounts of Chinese performance. These efforts counter concerns about the negative environmental impacts of Chinese outbound investment (whether discursively or through mitigation measures), and build Chinese-led institutions that engage on environmental issues in the context of broader developmental and security initiatives. An example of an SOE-led development cooperation initiative that fuses technocratic visions of a global renewable energy future with the resource and capacity of the Chinese state is the Global Energy Interconnection Development Cooperation Organization (GEIDCO), led by the China State Grid Corporation (Quimbre et al. 2023; Harlan 2025).

Other types of actors, such as subnational state actors or other ministries, have also become more active in recent years. For example, the Guizhou provincial government and Guiyang municipal government founded the Guiyang Eco-Forum in 2009 (Guiyang BEE 2024). The central government subsequently elevated it to the position of a "national-level global forum focusing on ecological civilization" in 2013. Various Chinese provinces and cities have signed memoranda of understanding with the CCCI, a collaborative initiative of California government and partners in China. China's general-purpose international cooperation initiatives have also begun to organize more frequent events on green development. For example, Chinese government and party-affiliated organizations have held an Understanding China conference annually since 2013. Originally seen as a "shadow G20" for "political luminaries interested in seriously discussing China's global role and implications," it has more recently been characterized as a stage-managed site

---

[11] This definition is a variation of the one adopted by Harlan and Lu (2022). Hard infrastructure aspects of China's green development cooperation (e.g., solar, wind) are discussed in Section 4 – Green Economic Statecraft.

for "propologue" (or propaganda as dialogue) (CMP 2024). The agenda for this conference has regularly featured speakers on the environment and green development.

Some green development cooperation efforts are also being implemented by civil society organizations. A full discussion of these efforts is beyond the scope of this Element, but research shows that Chinese civil society organizations exhibit a range of strategies (Xia 2024). Some operate quite closely to the state and actively engage in "civil diplomacy" (*minjian waijiao*), a Chinese state strategy to use Chinese civil society organizations to create more independent-seeming voices that present China-favorable messages. A few civil society organizations (typically based outside of China), such as Zhang Jingjing's Center for Transnational Environmental Accountability, take more confrontational approaches. Many other Chinese civil society organizations, such as the now-defunct Global Environmental Institute (GEI) and the Institute for Public & Environmental Affairs (IPE), navigate a space somewhere in between, seeking to conduct advocacy in ways that do not run afoul of the Chinese state, attempting to influence Chinese green agendas, and navigating the complexities of a relatively close, yet still independent, relationship to the Chinese state. International green groups have generally taken more moderate approaches in engaging with the Chinese state as well, seeking cooperative approaches based on dialogue, technical cooperation, or services provision. These groups are very active within some Chinese state development cooperation initiatives like CCICED and BRIGDC. The main exceptions are international human rights groups that have used more critical investigative and name-and-shame approaches to expose malfeasance by Chinese actors (CRI 2024; Wang 2022).

This section will present brief case studies of several green development cooperation efforts: (i) CCICED & BRIGDC; (ii) the case of the Kenya Standard Gauge Railway; and (iii) the LMEC.

CCICED and BRIGDC illustrate the shift in Chinese development cooperation over the last thirty years from China as a developing country recipient of assistance to a more proactive partner to the developed world and a provider of aid to the Global South. The Kenya SGR suggests conditions under which a Chinese SOE is more likely to respond to local environmental complaints; namely, under sustained pressure from more active local media and civil society. The LMEC presents a case where environmental issues have become a focus of intense geopolitical contestation with deep and unresolved divisions among potential winners and losers in the region. Different characterizations of what should be considered "environmental" and the appropriate balance between environment and development are central issues.

5.1 CCICED and BRIGDC

CCICED was established in 1992 (the year of the Rio Conference) as a high-level, multilateral platform for helping senior Chinese officials address China's burgeoning environmental challenges (Zhao & Hanson 2024). The Canadian International Development Agency was the lead donor with contributions from other countries such as Norway, Sweden, and the UK. Initial Chinese leadership included senior Chinese environmental officials, Qu Geping, Song Jian, and Xie Zhenhua. The platform's initial structure was indicative of its time, in which China sought advice and resources from the developed world. In addition to what China sought from the world, CCICED has also always provided a forum for Chinese leaders and researchers to convey messages to global environmental elites about Chinese progress on environmental protection. This has been particularly true in the Xi era of ecological civilization. CCICED has served as a point of contact for Chinese actors with the EU, the World Economic Forum, US EPA, UN officials, and others. In the Xi era, CCICED task forces have increasingly focused on China's global engagement. In 2016, it created a task force on South–South Cooperation for Ecological Civilization. In 2018, CCICED initiated a policy study on greening the Belt and Road Initiative.

BRIGDC is of much more recent vintage, launched at the Second Belt and Road Forum in April 2019 in Beijing and led by China's Ministry of Ecology and Environment and international partners. President Xi had proposed the BRIGDC two years before at the first BRI Forum in May 2017. BRIGDC is a global China-initiated multilateral institution with some 134 partners. The range of environmental issues and industrial sectors covered is as broad as the concept of green development itself, and includes green infrastructure, finance, governance, and a host of other issues. The stated purpose of BRIGDC is:

> [T]o promote international consensus, understanding, cooperation and concerted actions to achieve green development of BRI, to integrate sustainable development into the BRI through joint efforts, and to facilitate BRI participating countries to implement strong integration of environment and development elements of the SDGs (BRIGDC 2020a).

BRIGDC is meant to be a platform for policy dialogue and communication; environmental knowledge and information sharing; and green technology exchange and transfer. BRIGDC regularly produces policy reports and publishes the BRI Green Review. BRIGDC is a sophisticated institution that is more integrated into international networks than past Chinese cooperation efforts. For example, BRIGDC's inaugural executive director is Zhang Jianyu, an international environmental advocate who led the work of the U.S. Environmental Defense Fund in China for many years.

BRIGDC has been the subject of debates over whether it represents "green development or greenwashing" (Harlan 2021). BRIGDC is framed in the official rhetoric of Chinese development cooperation as a genuine effort at policy promotion and Chinese motivations for participation are described in altruistic or depoliticized pragmatic terms. BRIGDC has shown some potential to be a site of genuine information exchange, deliberation, and policy formation. For example, a December 2020 BRIGDC policy study proposed a "traffic light system" to "accelerate green and reduce brown investment" (BRIGDC 2020b). That policy report called for Chinese overseas investments to engage in green development by considering pollution control, climate change, and biodiversity protection. Most famously, it called for an exclusion list of projects not to be funded and a ranking of projects (red, yellow, green) according to environmental and social impact. It also called for projects to adhere to international environmental standards and to create grievance mechanisms for people and NGOs to use in the event of complaints. BRIGDC recommendations also encouraged Chinese companies to adhere to higher international or Chinese standards if host country rules are considered insufficient. These provisions were incorporated into MEE and MOFCOM Green Development Guidelines for Foreign Investment and Cooperation published in July 2021.

Critical accounts highlight the role of BRIGDC as mainly a symbolic effort to bolster "the BRI's reputation as a sustainable, win-win project" that "outweighs its practical contribution to environmental protection" (Geng & Lo 2023, p. 1181). More controversially, BRIGDC can serve as a forum for coopting global elites and persuading them of the legitimacy of Chinese environmental efforts. From the perspective of Chinese leadership, BRIGDC has a variety of advantages. It is a multilateral, but Chinese-led, body for transnational regulation that provides Chinese leaders with direct access to global environmental elites from the UN and other international organizations, major international civil society organizations, the environmental agencies in Global South countries, and major Chinese companies active in BRI projects. As a China-initiated governance institution, it symbolizes Chinese commitment to global goals of the Paris Agreement, the UN 2030 Sustainable Development Goals, and others. In contrast to CCICED, BRIGDC is increasingly framed in terms of China bringing lessons in green development to the world. BRIGDC also emerged in a period where Chinese leaders had begun to speak about strategic objectives to "perfect and reform the current international system" (Sun & Yu 2023). As an engagement-oriented, information-sharing body, it is a depoliticized space for addressing issues that have caused serious reputational damage to China and increased the risks of China's outbound investment and trade (Sun & Yu 2023, p. 101). It is not a forum where strong critics will likely have a voice. Its focus on dialogue, joint research, and voluntary standard setting in the context of a Chinese-led institution is cooperative in nature and generates little risk of unwanted pressures or constraints. The characteristics that make the forum appealing to Chinese leaders has generated skepticism from outside observers who see the messaging function of the institution as overriding its role in generating better environmental policy and outcomes (Geng & Lo 2023).

5.2 Kenya Standard Gauge Railway

In contrast to CCICED and BRIGDC, the multiphase Kenya Standard Gauge Railway (SGR) project offers an example of a project-specific response to environmental risks. The Kenya SGR is a $10 billion multiphase railway project. The first phase, completed in August 2017, extends from the port city of Mombasa westward through the capital city of Nairobi. Later phases of the project extend the SGR from Nairobi to Naivasha (completed in 2019), and from Naivasha to Malaba on the Uganda-Kenya border (Xia 2019). The Kenya SGR can be understood both as a response to local demand in Kenya and as a product of Chinese political economy dynamics; that is, China's Going Out policy as a "relocation of the domestic contradictions of capital accumulation" to Global South countries and a means of addressing China's domestic overcapacity problems (Huang & Lesutis 2023).

The main contractors for the project have been China Road and Bridge Corporation (CRBC) and its parent company China Communications Construction Company, one of China's largest central SOEs with significant business in BRI countries. The project is a key part of Kenya's national development program "Vision 2030." CRBC took the lead in securing the project with the Kenyan government and sought funding from China Export-Import Bank, which financed 90% of the initial phases of the project. In 2019, China Ex-Im Bank pulled its financial support for the project after the SGR was extended from Nairobi to Naivasha, due to concerns about the financial profitability of the project and the inability to come to terms on financing (CGSP 2025). As of early 2025, the project faced a revenue shortfall of US $7.8 million per month (Olander 2025). A newly announced public-private partnership deal between Chinese companies, China Ex-Im Bank, and the Kenyan government in April 2025 would revive the last phase of the project allowing it to connect to Uganda and bring it closer to the ultimate goal of connecting with mining regions of the Democratic Republic of Congo (CGSP 2025).

The project has been controversial on multiple fronts, including allegations of corruption and lack of transparency; concerns about cost and debt; economic harm to the trucking industry and ancillary economies around trucking routes that faced reduced business in the wake of the Kenya SGR; and adverse environmental impacts (Dahir 2022).

In the context of the non-environmental impacts of the project, Huang and Lesutis (2023, p. 1593) argue that the Chinese contractor responded to controversies over the SGR in ways that reflected the "hybridity" of the firm – that is, that it considered both its own profit motives and Chinese state concerns about China-Kenya diplomatic relationships, the role of the Kenyan SGR as a symbol of China's BRI, and that CRBC behavior would be perceived as representative of how "Chinese enterprises" behave beyond Chinese borders. They document how this resulted in the Chinese contractor taking unusually proactive steps in managing land acquisition and compensation and in agreeing to operate the SGR (eventually at a loss) because of pressure to ensure that the project was operated successfully and perceived as a success in the public eye. In another study, Li & Wang (2023) found that CRBC responded to local media reports criticizing CRBC's lack of operational transparency, racist treatment of workers, and harm to local Kenyan businesses through more proactive media engagement and public relations, as well as trainings for Chinese employees on anti-racism; in other words, a mix of public relations and substantive response to criticisms. These studies suggest that firms are willing to adapt to local pressures in the name of project success and mitigation of political and reputational risk. Li & Wang also contrast the relative responsiveness of CRBC in Kenyan to unresponsive Chinese SOEs in neighboring Ethiopia. They attribute the difference to more active local Kenyan media and civil society as compared to Ethiopia.

Chinese SOE responses to environmental concerns have reflected a similar kind of responsiveness; however, differing views of the proper relationship between development and the environment very much determine whether one sees such responses as acceptable or not. The Kenya SGR has been the subject of criticism regarding its environmental impacts as the project traverses several national parks. Identified impacts include ecosystem degradation from soil, water, and air contamination; soil erosion and flooding; introduction of invasive species; ecosystem fragmentation and destruction; and disturbance of movement patterns for wildlife through physical barriers, noise, and other pollution (Xia 2019; Okita-Ouma et al. 2021). China Ex-Im Bank carried out an environmental and social impact assessment prior to funding the project, considering pollution, health impacts, land acquisition needs, and forced resettlement. Local environmental groups brought several lawsuits against the project, arguing among other things that the project's environmental impact assessment did not adequately consider alternatives to mitigate environmental harms. This advocacy led to some project changes, such as elevation of segments of the railway to limit impacts on animal migration and some rerouting to bypass sensitive areas (Xia 2019).

Chinese accounts of the project perhaps unsurprisingly emphasize the environmental mitigation efforts and downplay ongoing environmental harms. For example, a BRIGDC book authored by a team affiliated with China's MEE, entitled *The Belt and Road Initiative Green Development Case Studies Report 2020*, contains a lead case study on the Nairobi-Malaba phase of the Kenyan SGR (BRIGDC 2022). It implicitly acknowledges environmental and labor criticisms by describing mitigation measures, such as the construction of an elevated "national park bridge" with noise barriers "to minimize the impact on wildlife," or the use of machine-made sand to avoid the need to dredge from local rivers. The BRIGDC case study makes no mention, however, of negative environmental impacts of earlier phases of the SGR, which bisected and exacerbated fragmentation in Kenya's Tsavo Conservation Area (Koskei et al., 2022; Lala et al., 2022; Okita-Ouma et al., 2021). It also does not grapple with other studies that have found the project's environmental mitigation measures to be inadequate (Jiang 2020). Underpasses designed to reduce habitat fragmentation and allow animal crossings are too few and far between and these areas are contaminated by oil, noise, and other pollution in a manner that has caused distress among native species such as African elephants (Okita-Ouma, et al. 2021). The barriers on elephant movement created by the SGR have also led to increased human-elephant conflict (Tsavo Trust 2025). The report also makes no mention of controversy (including litigation) over the siting of the SGR through Nairobi National Park, another key wildlife conservation area in Kenya (Mwangi et al. 2022; Lekalhaile undated). A different BRIGDC report authored by a group of Chinese and international experts is more candid about the known environmental problems of the Kenya SGR and offers more specific guidance on the range of environmental risks to consider, but it still omits discussion of concerns from independent researchers that mitigation measures have been inadequate (BRIGDC 2021, pp. 5–7, 42). A Xinhua report is the least circumspect about continuing environmental problems, declaring outright that the railway is "in harmony with wildlife conservation" (Xinhua 2022).

Ultimately, the Kenya SGR case represents a familiar conflict between development and the environment. Early stages of the project appeared to have generated the most serious impacts (e.g., insufficient passage for wildlife, continuing fragmentation of major ecosystems, exacerbation of human–wildlife conflict), but controversies like the passage of the SGR through Nairobi National Park have resulted in compromise and mitigation measures that improve on problems in the earlier phases of the project (e.g., by elevating the train to heights of 7.5 m to 41.5 m or installing sound barriers) while at the same time rejecting environmentalists' proposals to build outside of the park (Mwangi, et al. 2022; AFP 2018; personal observations).

At minimum, the case of the Kenya SGR is more complicated than it might seem at first blush. It is not obvious that Chinese firms are underperforming firms from other countries with similar projects or that the resultant measures are not a reasonable accommodation among competing considerations (development, environment, cost, timely completion, etc.). The routing of the Kenya SGR through Nairobi National Park, for example, may have been attractive to the government because it would require lesser amounts of land compensation as compared to alternative routes and less delay from negotiations with property owners (Wissenbach & Wang 2017). What's more, a 2024 Pew poll showed that high percentages of Kenyan respondents had strong or moderately favorable views of Chinese company impacts on the local economy, work to protect the environment, and treatment of local workers (Silver et al. 2024), suggesting that compromises by Chinese firms may have had a salutary effect on public opinion.

That said, for environmentalists, the Kenya SGR is but one component of a broader push to transform Kenya into a "newly-industrializing, middle-income country" that will create ever-growing pressure on the local environment and wildlife through more roads, railways, power plants, power lines, and real estate development (Mwangi et al. 2022). Overly positive statements from official Chinese media and incomplete discussion of environmental problems in BRIGDC materials create a sense that Chinese actors are unwilling to grapple with these larger dynamics or worse are engaged in obfuscation or greenwashing.

5.3 Lancang-Mekong Environmental Cooperation Center

I conclude with the case of the Lancang-Mekong Environmental Cooperation Center (LMEC). China established the LMEC in November 2017 as the environmental component of a broader regional cooperation mechanism among six countries along the Lancang/Mekong River basin (Cambodia, China, Laos, Myanmar, Thailand, and Vietnam) known as the Lancang-Mekong Cooperation (LMC) (Biba 2018; Geall 2019). The cooperation boasted Chinese state support from the highest levels: Premier Li Keqiang proposed the mechanism at the 1st Lancang-Mekong Cooperation Leaders' Meeting in Sanya in March 2016 and Chinese environmental vice-minister Huang Runqiu headlined the launch of the initiative in November 2017 (PRC MEE 2017). The LMC itself addresses a broader range of non-environmental issues under a "3+5 cooperation framework," which refers to three pillars and five priority areas for cooperation. The pillars are political and security issues; economic and sustainable development; and social, cultural and people-to-people exchanges. The priority areas are connectivity; production capacity; cross-border economic cooperation; water resources; agriculture; and poverty reduction.

The LMC/LMEC serves as a bellwether for several reasons. It is a case in which China holds significant power through its upstream position and its influence on the regional economy (Ho 2014). In the face of vociferous criticisms about environmental, social, and economic impacts, China has employed what is becoming a familiar composite strategy of developmental "carrots," depoliticization through dialogue and technocratic exchange, and the creation of a governance mechanism (the LMC/LMEC) that allows China to shape agendas and neutralize criticism. The region has also become a site of geopolitical competition with the LMC/LMEC gaining influence relative to more US-oriented institutions like the Mekong River Commission (MRC) or the Obama-era Lower Mekong Initiative (LMI) that later became the Trump-era Mekong-US Partnership (MUP).[12] The LMC/LMEC raises concerns about excessive Chinese influence, misinformation, and insufficient consideration of less powerful communities downstream. Yet, it is also an institution that has gained traction due to China's relative power and the comparatively modest impact of alternatives like the MRC or the LMI/MUP (Geall 2019; Johnson & Wongcha-Um 2020). How China manages tensions in the region from a position of relative power will offer insight into Chinese global environmentalism more broadly.

The source of environmental tension driving the creation of LMC/LMEC was China's construction of eleven mainstream dams and ninety-five tributary dams along the Lancang River (what China calls the portion of the Mekong River within its borders). China's stated motivations for dam construction have been economic development, flood and drought management, clean energy, and improvement of navigation. Critics of China's actions in the Lancang/Mekong watershed argue that Chinese dams are a threat to the natural environment and the livelihoods of tens of millions of people downstream. China's damming of the upper reaches of the Mekong impacts the downstream Mekong River watershed and has caused conflicts over Chinese control of downstream water supply, harms to fisheries and other ecosystems, and loss of soil fertility. Chinese dams trap significant amounts of sediment flow with negative impacts on agriculture and aquatic life in the Mekong Delta downstream (Ho 2014). The

---

[12] The Mekong River Commission (MRC), founded in 1995, is the only treaty-based river basin cooperation in the region. China is only a dialogue partner of the MRC. China is not a member or partner of the Lower Mekong Initiative or the US-Mekong Partnership.

most vocal critics have been Western governments and civil society, as well as local communities and environmentalists (Eyler 2020; ICG 2024, pp. 27–28).

Non-Chinese scholars have identified several aspects of the Chinese response to these controversies. I group these aspects into three categories: *geopolitical*, *economic*, and *environmental*.

Geopolitical. Biba (2018) argues that China was motivated to create the LMC/LMEC to increase its role in Mekong governance as a counter to US moves to build closer ties in the region and to find synergies with the broader objectives of other Chinese initiatives like the BRI and AIIB. Ha (2022) argues that China's active Mekong water diplomacy is driven by foreign policy objectives to "ensure a stable and friendly periphery in the basin and to manage the Mekong basin as a "new front for US-China rivalry in Southeast Asia."

This is consistent with how the US government sees the LMC/LMEC. US Secretary of State under Trump Mike Pompeo criticized China's upstream dams for concentrating control over downstream flows and warned ASEAN nations that the LMC was "a push to craft new Beijing-directed rules to govern the river" that would usurp the role of the Mekong River Commission, which received substantial funding from Western donors, or the Greater Mekong Subregion (GMS), a 1992 initiative of the Asian Development Bank (ADB) which received major funding from the US and Japan.

China has attempted to neutralize such concerns by framing the LMC/LMEC as a partnership among equals with shared objectives, rather than a situation with significant power imbalances in China's favor. According to Chinese environmental vice-minister Huang Runqiu, "[t]he Lancang and Mekong countries as developing countries share similar economic and environmental issues with China which is also a developing country. Our common goals are to share green experience, improve environmental quality, and promote the sustainable development of the countries concerned" (PRC MEE 2017).

Economic. The LMC/LMEC also seeks to depoliticize environmental controversies over Chinese dams by situating them in the broader context of economic development. As previously stated, the LMEC's environmental agenda is decentered by its placement among the five priority areas within the broader LMC, which focus heavily on economic development. China has promoted the developmental aspect of LMC through a contribution of more than US$300 million to an LMC Special Fund that has supported over 700 projects.[13] This approach of

---

[13] Compare this to the US $120 million the US contributed to the Obama-era LMI as of 2020 (Johnson & Wongcha-Um 2020). Official pronouncements about the Mekong-US Partnership do not indicate the amount of funding specifically earmarked for the MUP, but rather cite to "nearly $3.5 billion in assistance to the five Mekong partner countries" provided by the US Department of State and Agency for International Development (USAID) from 2009 to 2020 in areas such as

placing environmental considerations squarely within broader developmental discussions is a hallmark of Chinese global environmentalism. Further study is needed as to the actual economic benefits of these projects and the distribution of such benefits among different stakeholders.

Environmental. Regional actors, the US, and its allies view environmental issues related to China's water resource management and the impact of Chinese dams on lower Mekong nations as security issues (Quang & Borton 2023). China has in turn attempted to desecuritize these environmental issues by treating them as technical rather than political matters. Ha (2022) calls this a strategy of "moving issues off the security agenda" and "back into the realm of normal politics." For example, China has sought to legitimate its dam-building by emphasizing that the dams regulate the river's water flows and bring about benefits for "drought relief, water supply, navigation and ecology downstream." Ha (2022) also describes LMC study tours, visits and joint research studies that promote positive messages and shift blame for hydrologic changes from Chinese dams to more general factors like climate change.

China is also affirmatively reframing the environmental impacts of hydropower. China presents its dams as a source of low-carbon, renewable energy and downplays their well-documented ecological impacts – including impacts on sediment flows and water supply. Western environmentalists are almost uniformly opposed to large hydropower and are active in proposing economic and environmental pathways that do not require the construction of dams (see, e.g., Opperman et al. 2023). The LMC/LMEC has *not* been a forum where the propriety of dam construction is discussed, and it has been criticized for not sufficiently addressing the environmental and social impacts of dam construction. The Mekong River Commission, in contrast, has been more open in studying the negative effects of dams in the basin and has commissioned studies that recommend a moratorium on dam construction on the Mekong mainstream (ICEM 2010).

China has also challenged scientific research related to the dams. A 2019 US State Department-funded study (the "Eyes on Earth study") concluded, among other things, that Chinese dams were responsible for "severe lack of water in the Lower Mekong during the wet season of 2019." Brian Eyler, an American expert on China's dams on the Lancang River at the Stimson Center, put it more starkly, arguing that during the wet season of 2019, although China experienced normal to above average precipitation around its section of the Lancang/Mekong River, "its dams held back more water than ever – even as downstream countries suffered through an unprecedented wet season drought" (Eyler 2020). The study had a major

---

health, economic growth, peace and security, human rights and governance, education and social services, and humanitarian assistance (US Dept. of State. 2020).

impact on the discourse over China's actions in the Mekong as a comprehensive technical report with specific negative findings for China that received extensive media coverage and attention from government officials in the US and elsewhere. The MRC and others have criticized the report's methodology, "arguing that the research did not bear out the conclusions drawn by [Stimson Center commentary on the report and related] media reports" (ICG 2024). The Stimson Center acknowledged errors in the Eyes on Earth study but stood by the original assertions of Chinese dam impact based on new analysis with corrected data (Eyler et al. 2021). Chinese officials and state media, for their part, mounted an aggressive campaign to discredit the study (Shi 2020; Hu 2022; Hu & Zhao 2022; ICG 2024).

Chinese authorities have also faced intense criticism for insufficient public consultation with the downstream communities most affected by China's dams and inadequate information disclosure about dam water management practices. The lack of transparency has caused some to suspect the worst. Ho (2014, p. 8), for example, notes that China's "unilateral stance" on dam building brought criticism from lower riparian states that China was being "evasive and secretive." Chinese pledges to disclose more hydrologic data – such as the one Chinese Premier Li Keqiang made at the 3rd Lancang-Mekong Cooperation Leader's Meeting in August 2020 – are a good start (Li 2020; Shi 2020). However, it is worth noting that the pledge was only made in the wake of the Eyes on Earth report and Chinese MFA denials of the truth of that report (Hu & Lin 2020).

To summarize, China has presented the LMC/LMEC as a vehicle for negotiating a win-win developmental and environmental situation in the region. The US has instead treated the LMC/LMEC as a Chinese powerplay with increasingly dire results for the local environment. Regional governments and businesses have been more willing to explore the developmental opportunities associated with dams, whereas local fishing and agricultural communities and environmentalists are more concerned about bearing a disproportionate share of the negative impacts of dams. How Mekong actors respond to China's overtures in the region are likely influenced by the leverage China holds as their most important trading partner (Johnson & Wongcha-Um 2020), but it will also be affected by the alternatives available to them. Geall (2019) notes that competing Mekong initiatives from Japan, India, Thailand, Australia, and the US "pale in comparison with the scale and speed of China's expansion down the Mekong." Given the weakness of alternatives, downstream governments, which have generally been interested in exploiting hydropower (ICG 2024), may choose to engage with China's offer of development and security benefits, even in the face of serious environmental harms.

* * * * *

The governments of the developed world have long acted as donors and implementers in the world of international development cooperation. The US, Germany, UK, EU, Japan, and France are among the top contributors these days. China has long been a recipient and beneficiary of aid. We recounted in Section 2 how pro-environmental factions within China built ties with the international community beginning in the 1980s to obtain financial resources, expertise, and capacity support. With the rise of Chinese global environmentalism, China has moved from being a recipient of development support toward being a provider.

China's environmental development cooperation seems to be motivated by domestic and global reputational concerns, a desire to mitigate environmental risks of Chinese outbound investment and trade, and the goals of demonstrating Chinese global leadership and strengthening diplomatic ties. These cooperative mechanisms signal Chinese commitment to addressing environmental problems that have brought on global criticism and controversy, and they reflect genuine environmental progress at times. However, the sheer scale of Chinese environmental impacts, power imbalances, and indications that these efforts are more greenwashing than genuine substance has led to mixed responses to Chinese development cooperation among relevant audiences.

6 Conclusion

This Element has sought to add nuance to ongoing debates about China's global environmental impacts and its forays into green development around the world. This examination of Chinese global environmentalism leads us to several conclusions.

First, China's promotion of Chinese global environmentalism is a strategic effort motivated primarily by economic development and security objectives. It is a means of managing the environmental, social, and political risks of Chinese global trade and investment, and an attempt to capture the economic and political benefits of green development. As an affirmative effort, it is closely tied to notions of "high-quality development" (*gao zhiliang fazhan*) and "new productive forces" (*xin zhisheng chanli*) that have been ascendant in China during the Xi era. It is also a way to deal with domestic overcapacity in various green industries. In this way, it shares some features with the developmental environmentalism seen in neighboring countries like Japan and Korea but given China's size and the scope of its ambitions it is also something broader with greater geopolitical implications.

Second, in Chinese global environmentalism, we see a powerful confluence of environmental, development, and security goals that render it more likely some environmental goals will be met. This is particularly true in the context of clean energy manufacturing and deployment, where Chinese strategic objectives align in a way that will likely drive rapid clean energy deployment. It also means, however, that environmental goals or norms that do not enjoy such confluence will more likely be given short shrift. Notions of environmentalism that emphasize reduced consumption, for example, have little chance of making it onto a Chinese-led global environmental agenda (though this is also true for developed nation environmental agendas).

Third, China's emergence as a major global environmental player will reinforce some existing norms of global environmentalism and challenge others. China's push for green development aligns itself with global approaches that bring together environmental and developmental goals, such as the Green New Deal or policies based on "sustainable development." This push has been framed as supportive of Paris Agreement goals, norms of CBDR, and UN Sustainable Development Goals. In other respects, Chinese approaches are already altering global norms – such as in the growing acceptance of green industrial policy and the enhanced role of the state in accelerating deployment of clean energy. It reinforces the idea that a strong, technocratic state is essential to successful performance.

Fourth, Chinese global environmentalism also gains in strength from the inadequacies in current Western responses to global environmental and developmental needs. In some instances, China gains purchase by merely performing no worse than other major powers on environmental matters. This is hardly an inspiring thought, but sooner or later it will become apparent that Western observers have been criticizing China more harshly for the same sorts of things they have done themselves.

An increasingly assertive China is also now making the case that it is surpassing the West in important ways, such as in Chinese dominance in clean technology development and in the sense that the West is either neglecting the Global South or imposing "rules for thee, but not for me." Indeed, the growing contrast with the US could not be sharper. As of this writing, at the start of the second Trump term, the US has taken on broadly anti-environmental stances and is instituting aggressive policies to roll back climate action, limit the expansion of renewable energy and electric vehicles, and even block the most basic standards of energy and water efficiency. The US has also drastically cut back on foreign aid, leaving China with a clear path to build ties with the Global South through green development cooperation or otherwise. Moreover, while liberal democratic values have historically been a leading source of global legitimacy for the US and EU, as of this writing, Donald Trump is aggressively pushing US politics in an illiberal direction and far right political parties are ascendant throughout Europe. Such illiberal, anti-environmental views are not supported by substantial numbers of people in the US. For example, the US

Climate Alliance is an organization supported by governors representing 54% of the US population and 57% of the US economy that advocates for US climate action. It nonetheless represents the position of the US government during Republican administrations.

Fifth, China's insistence on narratives that emphasize "top-down design" is a double-edged sword. This is part of Chinese image making – projecting strength and charisma at the top capable of delivering development and security. But in seemingly suggesting that all policy emanates from the black box of China's leadership, it is also creating a rising sense of threat or risk in the rest of the world. This aspect of China's official narrative also reinforces concerns about the illiberal aspects of Chinese governance, including information control and tight regulation of free speech, political organization, and other civil rights. What's more, this also masks a sprawling bureaucratic planning process that has been surprisingly effective in incorporating wide-ranging input and generating policy-oriented, pragmatic responses to different risks as they have emerged (Wang 2018b). These processes are messier and less predictable than Chinese leaders like to admit, but they also reflect a level of responsiveness and accountability that global audiences would perhaps find comforting if they were able to look behind the veil of Chinese propaganda.

Ultimately, China has made tremendous strides in environmental governance that are beginning to reshape the way the nation is understood in developed countries, the Global South, and within China. China's system of governance has been able to achieve rational public-minded policy objectives to mitigate environmental harms, despite substantial obstacles and missteps along the way. At the same time, China's developmental approach to environmentalism raises a host of unanswered questions that continue to generate controversies around the world. Chinese actions are continuing to place extraordinary pressure on the natural environment, and Chinese environmentalism has no more attained the perfect harmony between man and nature than efforts at sustainable development before it – no matter what official Chinese accounts would have us believe (Xinhua 2022). Moreover, certain aspects of China's approach to environmentalism – insufficient transparency and participation, a tendency toward coercion, an unwillingness to openly admit to error – continue to generate substantial concerns beyond China's borders and erode trust. Those in the rest of the world should rightly wonder if these illiberal tendencies will only increase as China's power grows. Greater Chinese efforts to improve environmental performance and promote transparency, public participation, and compromise – even in the face of democratic backsliding in the developed world – would go a long way toward improving China's global standing. Whether China will take advantage of these opportunities remains to be seen. It has already made inroads, but it still has a long way to go.

Bibliography

Adam, B. et al. (2024). Emissions of HFC-23 Do Not Reflect Commitments Made Under the Kigali Amendment, *Communications Earth & Environment*, www.nature.com/articles/s43247-024-01946-y.

Agence France Press (AFP) (Mar. 1, 2018). Anger as Rail Construction Begins in Nairobi National Park, *The East African*, https://www.theeastafrican.co.ke/tea/news/east-africa/anger-as-rail-construction-begins-in-nairobi-national-park-1385094.

Alford, W. P. & Y. Y. Shen (1997). Limits of the Law in Addressing China's Environmental Dilemma, *Stanford Environmental Law Journal*, 16(1), 125–148.

Allan, B., et al. (2018). The Distribution of Identity and the Future of International Order: China's Hegemonic Prospects, *International Organization*, 72(4), 839–869.

Atlantic Council (2023). A Conversation with General Laura J. Richardson on Security Across the Americas, https://www.youtube.com/watch?v=S2ry5Xl7AhM&t=598s.

Bartlett, J. (2024). Copper, Pragmatism, and Going Green: A History of Chile-China Relations, *Dialogue Earth*, https://dialogue.earth/en/business/390865-copper-pragmatism-and-going-green-a-history-of-chile-china-relations/.

Beeson, M. (2010). The Coming of Environmental Authoritarianism, *Environmental Politics*, 19(2), 276–294.

BBC (2019). Kenya Halts Lamu Coal Power Project at World Heritage Site, https://www.bbc.com/news/world-africa-48771519.

Biba, S. (2018). China's "Old" and "New" Mekong River Politics: the Lancang-Mekong Cooperation from a Comparative Benefit-Sharing Perspective, *Water International*, 43(5), 622–641.

Boyd, O. (2012). China's Energy Reform and Climate Policy: the Ideas Motivating Change, *Australia National University Working Paper*, https://ideas.repec.org/p/ags/ancewp/249396.html.

Brain, S. & V. Pál eds. (2019). *Environmentalism under Authoritarian Regimes: Myth, Propaganda, Reality*, Routledge.

BRI International Green Development Coalition (BRIGDC) (2020a). *Overview*, http://en.brigc.net/About_us/Overview/202009/t20200928_102502.html [https://perma.cc/EYN4-6QTR].

BRIGDC (2020b). *Green Development Guidance for BRI Projects Baseline Study Report*, http://en.brigc.net/Reports/Report_Download/2020/202012/P020210202120471013629.pdf.

BRIGDC (2021). *Green Development Guidance for BRI Projects Phase II Task 2: Guide for Key BRI Sectors Highways and Railways*, http://en.brigc.net/Reports/Report_Download/2021/202110/P020211025599530110826.pdf.

BRIDGC (2022). *The Belt and Road Initiative Green Development Case Studies Report 2020*, http://en.brigc.net/Reports/research_subject/202011/P020201129780236943177.pdf.

Buckley, C. & H. Fountain (2018). In a High-Stakes Environmental Whodunit, Many Clues Point to China, *NY Times*, www.nytimes.com/2018/06/24/world/asia/china-ozone-cfc.html.

Buckley, C. & H. Fountain (2021). China's Emissions of Ozone-Harming Gas Are Declining, Studies Find, *NY Times*, www.nytimes.com/2021/02/10/climate/ozone-layer-china-cfcs.html.

Buckley, C. (2010). China Calls US a Pig in the Mirror on Climate Change, *Reuters*, https://www.reuters.com/article/world/china-calls-u-s-a-pig-in-the-mirror-on-climate-change-idUSTRE6980NX/.

Cai, S. & M. Voigts (1994). The Development of China's Environmental Diplomacy, *Pacific Rim Law and Policy Journal*, 3, S-17–42.

Canbero, F. & D.B. Solomon (2024). Chile Lithium Projects Garner Interest from Over 50 Companies, *Reuters*, https://www.reuters.com/markets/commodities/over-50-companies-express-interest-developing-chile-lithium-projects-2024-06-18/.

Carbon Brief (2024). Analysis: China's Emissions Have Now Caused More Global Warming than EU, www.carbonbrief.org/analysis-chinas-emissions-have-now-caused-more-global-warming-than-eu/.

Carothers, C. & J. Freedman (2025). America the Failure? Critical Narratives of the United States in Chinese State Media, *China Quarterly*, 262, 482–498.

Chen, L. & B. Naughton (2016). An Institutionalized Policy-Making Mechanism: China's Return to Techno-Industrial Policy, *Research Policy*, 45(10), 2138–2152.

China Media Project (CMP) (2024). *What Does It Mean to Understand China?*, https://chinamediaproject.org/2024/01/04/what-does-it-mean-to-understand-china/.

China Global South Project (CGSP) (2025). New Deal Revives Kenya's Standard Gauge Railway, https://chinaglobalsouth.com/2025/04/08/new-deal-revives-kenyas-standard-gauge-railway/.

Climate Rights Int'l (CRI) (2024). *Nickel Unearthed: The Human and Climate Costs of Indonesia's Nickel Industry*, https://cri.org/reports/nickel-unearthed/.

Coenen, J., S. Bager, P. Meyfroidt, J. New & E. Challies (2020). Environmental Governance of China's Belt and Road Initiative, *Envt'l Policy and Governance*, 31(1), 3–17.

Congressional-Executive Commission on China (CECC) (2023a). *Implementation of the Uyghur Forced Labor Prevention Act and the Impact on Global Supply Chains*, www.cecc.gov/events/hearings/implementation-of-the-uyghur-forced-labor-prevention-act-and-the-impact-on-global.

CECC (2023b) *Hearing Materials – From Cobalt to Cars: How China Exploits Child and Forced Labor in the Congo*, www.cecc.gov/events/hearings/from-cobalt-to-cars-how-china-exploits-child-and-forced-labor-in-the-congo.

Chilean Government, Ministry of Energy (2022). *National Electromobility Strategy*, https://www.gob.cl/en/news/national-electromobility-strategy-launch-government-announces-only-electric-vehicles-will-be-sold-chile-2035/.

Conrad, B. (2012). China in Copenhagen: Reconciling the Beijing "Climate Revolution" and the "Copenhagen Climate Obstinacy," *China Quarterly*, 210, 435–455.

Dahir, A.L. (Aug. 7, 2022). "Jewel in the Crown of Corruption": The Troubles of Kenya's China-Funded Train, *NY Times*, https://www.nytimes.com/2022/08/07/world/africa/kenya-election-train.html.

Davidson, M., et al. (2022). Risks of Decoupling from China on Low-Carbon Technologies, *Science*, 377, 1266–1269.

Davidson, M., et al. (2023). Hard to Say Goodbye: South Korea, Japan, and China as the Last Lenders for Coal, *Envt'l Politics*, 32(7), 1186–1207.

Delgado, O. & P. Logiodice (2025). Chile Can Pave the Way to Clean Transport in Latin America, *ICCT*, https://theicct.org/chile-can-help-pave-the-way-to-clean-transport-in-latin-america-mar25/.

Economy, E. (1998). "China's Environmental Diplomacy," in *China and the World: Chinese Foreign Policy Faces the New Millennium* (Samuel S. Kim ed.).

Economy, E. (2004). *The River Runs Black: The Environmental Challenge to China's Future*, Cornell University Press.

Economy, E. & M. Levi (2014). *By All Means Necessary*, Oxford University Press.

Environmental Investigation Agency (EIA) UK (2013). *Two Billion Tonne Climate Bomb: How to Defuse the HFC-23 Problem*, https://eia-international.org/report/the-two-billion-tonne-climate-bomb-how-to-defuse-the-hfc-23-problem/.

EIA UK (2018). *Blowing It: Illegal Production and Use of Banned CFC-11 in China's Foam Blowing Industry*, https://eia.org/report/20180709-blowing-it-illegal-production-and-use-of-banned-cfc-11-in-chinas-foam-blowing-industry/.

EIA UK (2022). *Chemical Nightmare: Ending Emissions of Fluorochemical Greenhouse Gases*, https://eia-international.org/report/chemical-nightmare-ending-emissions-of-fluorochemical-greenhouse-gases/.

EIA UK (2024). *Unchecked: The Flourochemical Industry's Scandalous HFC-23 By-Product Emissions Amid the Climate Crisis*, https://eia-international.org/wp-content/uploads/2024-EIA-UK-Unchecked-HFC-23-Climate-Briefing-SPREADS.pdf/.

Eyler, B., et al. (2020). New Evidence: How China Turned Off the Tap on the Mekong River, *Stimson Center*, www.stimson.org/2020/new-evidence-how-china-turned-off-the-mekong-tap/.

Eyler, B., et al. (2021). Consultative Processes Lead to More Accurate Monitoring of the Mekong from Eyes on Earth and the Stimson Center, *Stimson Center*, www.stimson.org/2021/consultative-processes-lead-to-more-accurate-monitoring-of-the-mekong-from-eyes-on-earth-and-the-stimson-center/.

Fuentes, V. (2020). Chilean Lawmakers Push for Restrictions on Chinese Buying Spree, *Bloomberg News*, https://financialpost.com/pmn/business-pmn/chilean-lawmakers-push-for-restrictions-on-chinese-buying-spree.

Gallagher, K. S. (2014). *The Globalization of Clean Energy Technology: Lessons from China*, MIT Press.

Gallagher, K. S. & Q. Qi (2021). Chinese Overseas Investment Policy: Implications for Climate Change, *Global Policy*, 12(3), 260–272.

Gao, X. & J. Teets (2020). Civil Society Organizations in China: Navigating the Local Government for More Inclusive Environmental Governance, *China Information*, 35(1), 46–66.

Gao, C., et al. (2021). Volcanic Climate Impacts Can Act as Ultimate and Proximate Causes of Chinese Dynastic Collapse, *Communications Earth & Environment*, 234, 1–11.

Gare, A. (2017). *The Philosophical Foundations of Ecological Civilization: A Manifesto for the Future*, Routledge.

Geall, S. (2019). Troubles on the Mekong, *Foreign Affairs*, www.foreignaffairs.com/articles/china/2019-11-07/troubles-mekong.

Geall, S. & A. Ely (2018). Narratives and Pathways Towards an Ecological Civilization in Contemporary China, *China Quarterly*, 236, 1175–1196.

Geng, Q. & K. Lo (2023). China's Green Belt and Road Initiative: Transnational Environmental Governance and Causal Pathways of Orchestration, *Environmental Politics*, 32(7), 1163–1185.

Gilley, B. (2012). Authoritarian Environmentalism and China's Response to Climate Change, *Environmental Politics*, 21(2), 281–307.

Goron, C. (2018). Ecological Civilisation and the Political Limits of the Chinese Concept of Sustainability, *China Perspectives*, 4, 39–52.

Graham, J., et al. (2021). How China Beat the US in Electric Vehicle Manufacturing, *Issues in Science and Technology*, https://issues.org/china-us-electric-vehicles-batteries/.

Green-Weiskel, L. (2022). *Cooperation or Competition with China: Interest Groups and US Policy on Climate Change*, dissertation, City University of New York, https://academicworks.cuny.edu/gc_etds/4864/.

Guiyang Bureau of Ecology & Environment (Guiyang BEE) (2024). 2024 Eco Forum Global Guiyang Paves Way for Greener Future, http://sthjj.english.guiyang.gov.cn/2024-10/08/c_1029822.htm [https://perma.cc/XE5F-UBDE].

Ha, H. T. (2022). China's Hydro-politics Through the Lancang-Mekong Cooperation, *ISEAS Perspective*, www.iseas.edu.sg/articles-commentaries/iseas-perspective/2022-116-chinas-hydro-politics-through-the-lancang-mekong-cooperation-by-hoang-thi-ha/.

Hale, T., et al. (2020). Belt and Road Decision-Making in China and Recipient Countries: How and to What Extent Does Sustainability Matter? *ISEP & BSG Report*.

Hansen, M., et al. (2018). Ecological Civilization: Interpreting the Chinese Past, Projecting the Global Future, *Global Environmental Change*, 53, 195–203.

Harlan, T. (2025). China's Green Cooperation in the Energy Sector: Overview and Analysis, *Pacific Basin Law Journal*.

Harlan, T. (2021). Green Development or Greenwashing? A Political Ecology Perspective on China's Green Belt and Road, *Eurasian Geography and Economics*, 61, 1–25.

Harlan, T. & J. Lu (2022). Green Cooperation: Environmental Governance and Development Aid on the Belt and Road, *Wilson Center*, www.wilsoncenter.org/sites/default/files/media/uploads/documents/Harlan%20and%20Lu_Green%20Cooperation.pdf.

Harvey, F. (2025). Xi Contrasts China's Clean Energy Promises with Trump Turmoil, *The Guardian*, https://www.theguardian.com/environment/2025/apr/23/un-chief-no-group-or-government-can-stop-clean-energy-future.

Hawkins, A. (2023). Biden Confronts Deep Skepticism of US Agenda in Latin America, *Politico*.

He D., et al. (2022). Report 2021 CWEA - *IEA Wind TCP*, https://iea-wind.org/wp-content/uploads/2022/12/IEA_Wind_TCP_AR2021_CWEA.pdf.

Hilton, I. (2024). How China Became the World's Leader on Renewable Energy, *Yale Environment*, 360, https://e360.yale.edu/features/china-renewable-energy.

Ho, S. (2014). River Politics: China's Policies in the Mekong and the Brahmaputra in Comparative Perspective, *Journal of Contemporary China*, 86, 1–20.

Hou, L. (2024) China Praised for Climate Financial Aid, *China Daily*, www.chinadaily.com.cn/a/202411/18/WS673a96d4a310f1265a1cdf94.html [https://perma.cc/9M9M-FY2P].

Hou, Q. (2023). Envoy Calls for More Joint Efforts on Climate Action, *China Daily*, www.chinadaily.com.cn/a/202312/11/WS65765057a31040ac301a70d2.html [https://perma.cc/NJ8C-MXU9].

Hou, Q. (2024). China has Signed 53 MOUs on South-South Climate Cooperation with 42 Countries, *China Daily*, www.chinadaily.com.cn/a/202411/06/WS672b381aa310f1265a1cbda3.html [https://perma.cc/2S8D-RR2L].

Hove, A. (2024). Clean Energy Innovation in China: Fact and Fiction, and Implication for the Future, *Oxford Institute for Energy Studies*, www.oxfordenergy.org/publications/clean-energy-innovation-in-china-fact-and-fiction-and-implications-for-the-future/.

Hu, Y. (2022). Chinese Experts Find Apparent Errors in Biased Data on Chinese Dams on Mekong River by US-funded Project, *Global Times*, www.globaltimes.cn/page/202203/1253764.shtml.

Hu, Y. & X. Lin (2020). US Smear Campaign Against Mekong River Dams Riddled with Loopholes, *Global Times*, www.globaltimes.cn/page/202009/1201107.shtml.

Hu Y. & J. Zhao (2022). GT Investigates: Who Are the Mouthpieces of US-Led War of Public Opinion on "Chinese Dams' Threats" Along Mekong River, and What Are Their Typical Methods? *Global Times*, www.globaltimes.cn/page/202203/1257016.shtml.

Huang, C., et al. (2024). Americans Remain Critical of China, *Pew Research Center*, www.pewresearch.org/global/2024/05/01/americans-remain-critical-of-china/.

Huang, C., et al. (2025). Negative Views of China Have Softened Slightly Among Americans, *Pew Research Center*, www.pewresearch.org/global/2025/04/17/negative-views-of-china-have-softened-slightly-among-americans/.

Huang, Z. & G. Lesutis (2023). Improvised Hybridity in the "Fixing" of Chinese Infrastructure Capital: The Case of Kenya's Standard Gauge Railway, *Antipode*, 55(5), 1587–1607.

Int'l Center for Environmental Management (ICEM) (2010). *Strategic Environmental Assessment of Hydropower on the Mekong Mainstream (Final Report) – Prepared for the Mekong River Commission*, https://icem.com.au/documents/envassessment/mrc_sea_hp/SEA_Final_Report_Oct_2010.pdf.

Int'l Crisis Group (ICG) (2024). Dammed in the Mekong: Averting an Environmental Catastrophe, www.crisisgroup.org/asia/south-east-asia/cambodia-thailand-china/343-dammed-mekong-averting-environmental-catastrophe.

Int'l Energy Agency (IEA) (2022). *Special Report on Solar PV Global Supply Chains*, www.iea.org/reports/solar-pv-global-supply-chains.

IEA (2023). *Energy Technology Perspectives 2023*, www.iea.org/reports/energy-technology-perspectives-2023.

IEA (2024a). *Global Critical Minerals Outlook 2024*, www.iea.org/reports/global-critical-minerals-outlook-2024.

IEA (2024b). *Global EV Outlook 2024*, www.iea.org/reports/global-ev-outlook-2024.

International Institute for Sustainable Development (IISD) (2024). Daily Report for 29 October 2024, 13th Meeting of the Conference of the Parties to the Vienna Convention for the Protection of the Ozone Layer (COP13) and 36th Meeting of the Parties to the Montreal Protocol on Substances that Deplete the Ozone Layer (MOP36), https://enb.iisd.org/montreal-protocol-ozone-mop36-vienna-convention-cop13-daily-report-29oct2024.

Institute for Governance & Sustainable Development (IGSD) (2024). HFC-23 China Policy Brief, www.igsd.org/hfc-23-china-policy-brief/.

Jahiel, A. (1998). The Organization of Environmental Protection in China, *China Quarterly*, 156, 757–787.

Jamasmie, C. (2018). China Says Chile Move to Block $5bn SQM Lithium Deal Could Be Harmful, *Mining.com*, https://www.mining.com/china-says-chile-move-to-block-5bn-sqm-lithium-deal-could-be-harmful/.

Jiang, F. (2020), Chinese Contractor Involvement in Wildlife Protection in Africa: Case Study of Mombasa-Nairobi Standard Gauge Railway Project, Kenya, *Land Use Policy*, 95, 104650.

Johnson, K. & P. Wongcha-Um (2020). Water Wars: Mekong River Another Front in U.S.-China Rivalry, *Reuters*, www.reuters.com/article/business/

environment/water-wars-mekong-river-another-front-in-us-china-rivalry-idUSKCN24P0K6/.

Johnson, T., et al. (1997). Clear Water, Blue Skies: China's Environment in the New Century, *World Bank*, https://documents.worldbank.org/en/publication/documents-reports/documentdetail/944011468743999953/clear-water-blue-skies-chinas-environment-in-the-new-century.

Kennedy, J. (2012). Environmental Protests in China on Dramatic Rise, Expert Says, *South China Morning Post*, https://www.scmp.com/news/china/article/1072407/environmental-protests-china-rise-expert-says.

Kong, B. (2019). *Modernization Through Globalization: Why China Finances Foreign Policy Energy Projects Worldwide*, Palgrave Macmillan, https://link.springer.com/book/10.1007/978-981-13-6016-9.

Kong, B. & K. P. Gallagher (2021). The New Coal Champion of the World: The Political Economy of Chinese Overseas Development Finance for Coal-fired Power Plants, *Energy Policy*, 155, 112334.

Koskei, M., et al (2022). The Role of Environmental, Structural and Anthropogenic Variables on Underpass Use by African Savanna Elephants (*Loxodonta Africana*) in the Tsavo Conservation Area, *Global Ecology & Conservation*, 38, e02199.

Lala, F., et al (2022). Influence of Infrastructure, Ecology, and Underpass-Dimensions on Multi-Year Use of Standard Gauge Railway Underpasses by Mammals in Tsavo, Kenya. *Sci Rep* 12, 5698.

Lee, C. K. (2022). Global China at 20: Why, How and So What? *China Quarterly*, 250, 313–331.

Lekalhaile, K. (undated). Building the SGR Inside the Park is Wrong, *Africa Network for Animal Welfare*, https://www.anaw.org/index.php/media-briefs/building-the-sgr-inside-the-park-is-wrong.

Lewis, J. (2012). *Green Innovation in China: China's Wind Power Industry and the Global Transition to a Low-Carbon Economy*, Columbia University Press.

Li, H. & Y. Wang (2023). African Media Cultures and Chinese Public Relations Strategies in Kenya and Ethiopia, *Carnegie Endowment for International Peace*, https://carnegieendowment.org/research/2023/02/african-media-cultures-and-chinese-public-relations-strategies-in-kenya-and-ethiopia.

Li, K. (August 24, 2020). Full Text: Speech by Premier Li Keqiang at the Third Lancang-Mekong Cooperation Leaders' Meeting, *Xinhua*, https://english.www.gov.cn/premier/speeches/202008/25/content_WS5f4448cac6d0f7257693ae42.html [https://perma.cc/2DRU-VY7L].

Li, Y. & J. Shapiro (2020). *China Goes Green: Coercive Environmentalism for a Troubled Planet*, Polity.

Liu, C., et al. (2022). Explaining the Energy Mix in China's Electricity Projects Under the Belt and Road Initiative, *Environmental Politics*, 32, 1117–1139.

Liu, J. & J. Diamond (2005). China's Environment in a Globalizing World, *Nature*, 435, 1179–1186, www.nature.com/articles/4351179a.

Lu, J. & T. Harlan (2021). COP15 in Kunming: A New Role for China in Global Conservation? *Asia Dispatches*, www.wilsoncenter.org/blog-post/cop15-kunming-new-role-china-global-conservation.

Lu, Y. & W. Han (2025). China's BYD, Tsingshan Scrap Plans for Chile Lithium Plants as Price Collapses, *Caixin*, https://www.caixinglobal.com/2025-05-09/chinas-byd-tsingshan-scrap-plans-for-chile-lithium-plants-as-price-collapses-102317742.html.

Lynas, M. (2009). How Do I Know China Wrecked the Copenhagen Deal? I Was in the Room, *The Guardian*, www.theguardian.com/environment/2009/dec/22/copenhagen-climate-change-mark-lynas.

Ma, X. & L. Ortolano (2000). *Environmental Regulation in China: Institutions, Enforcement, and Compliance*, Lanham.

Mearsheimer, J. (2021). The Inevitable Rivalry: America, China, and the Tragedy of Great-Power Politics, *Foreign Affairs*, www.foreignaffairs.com/articles/china/2021-10-19/inevitable-rivalry-cold-war.

Mercator Institute for China Studies (MERICS) (2022). Chile's Once-Pioneering Relationship with China is Turning into Dependency, https://merics.org/en/chiles-once-pioneering-relationship-china-turning-dependency.

Montzka, S., et al. (2018). An Unexpected and Persistent Increase in Global Emissions of Ozone-Depleting CFC-11, *Nature*, 557, 413–417.

Myllyvirta, L. & E. Howard (2018). Five Things We Learned from the World's Biggest Air Pollution Database, *Unearthed*, https://unearthed.greenpeace.org/2018/05/02/air-pollution-cities-worst-global-data-world-health-organisation/.

Myllyvirta, L. (2023). China Permits Two New Coal Power Plants Per Week in 2022, *Center for Research on Energy and Clean Air*, https://energyandcleanair.org/publication/china-permits-two-new-coal-power-plants-per-week-in-2022/.

Myllyvirta, L. (2024). Clean Energy Was Top Driver of China's Economic Growth in 2023, *Carbon Brief*, www.carbonbrief.org/analysis-clean-energy-was-top-driver-of-chinas-economic-growth-in-2023/.

Mwangi, F., et al (2022). Development Challenges and Management Strategies on the Kenyan National Park System: A Case of Nairobi National Park, *Int'l Journal of Geoheritage and Parks*, 10(1), 16–26.

Nahm, J. (2021). *Collaborative Advantage: Forging Green Industries in the New Global Economy*, Oxford University Press.

Naughton, B. (2005). The New Common Economic Program: China's Eleventh Five-Year Plan and What It Means, *China Leadership Monitor*, 16, 1–10, www.hoover.org/sites/default/files/uploads/documents/clm16_bn.pdf.

Nedopil, C. (2021). Green Finance for Soft Power: An Analysis of China's Green Policy Signals and Investments in the Belt and Road Initiative, *Environmental Policy and Governance*, 32(2), 85–97.

Nedopil, C. (2023). Lessons from China's Overseas Coal Exit and Domestic Support, *Science*, 379(6637), 1084–1087.

Nedopil, C. (2025). China Belt and Road Initiative (BRI) Investment Report 2024, https://greenfdc.org/china-belt-and-road-initiative-bri-investment-report-2024/.

Nedopil, C. & M. Yue (2024). Does Green Overseas Investment Improve Public Perception in Host Countries? Evidence from Chinese Energy Engagement in 32 African Countries, *Sustainability*, 16(2), 590.

Nemet, G. (2019). *How Solar Energy Became Cheap: A Model for Low-Carbon Innovation*, Routledge.

Nye, J. (2004). *Soft Power: The Means to Success in World Politics*, Public Affairs.

Okita-Ouma, B., et al. (2021). Effectiveness of Wildlife Underpasses and Culverts in Connecting Elephant Habitats: a Case Study of New Railway through Kenya's Tsavo National Parks *African Journal of Ecology*, 59(3), 624–640.

Oksenberg, M. & E. Economy (1999). *China Joins the World: Progress and Prospects*, Council on Foreign Relations.

Olander, E. (2025). China Touts Success of Kenya's Standard Gauge Railway But Leaves Out One Very Important Detail, *China Global South Project*, https://chinaglobalsouth.com/2025/03/10/china-touts-success-of-kenyas-standard-gauge-railway-but-leaves-out-one-very-important-detail/.

Opperman, J., et al. (2019). *Connected and Flowing: a Renewable Future for Rivers, Climate and People*. WWF & The Nature Conservancy, https://www.worldwildlife.org/publications/connected-flowing-a-renewable-future-for-rivers-climate-and-people.

Osborn, C. (2023). Germany's Scholz Calls for a New Approach to the Lithium Rush, *Foreign Policy*, https://foreignpolicy.com/2023/02/03/scholz-germany-argentina-brazil-chile-lithium-energy-ukraine-weapons/.

Park H., et al. (2023). A Rise in HFC-23 Emissions from Eastern Asia Since 2015, *Atmospheric Chemistry and Physics*, 23(16), 9401–9411.

People's Daily (Feb. 19, 2025). Vigorously Promote the High-quality Development of China's New Energy (*dali tuidong woguo xinnengyuan gaozhiliang fazhan*), http://www.news.cn/politics/20250219/e65246cd22c94494a3c30c09c6227d1d/c.html [https://perma.cc/B7SX-8TGJ].

People's Republic of China (PRC) (2022). *China's Achievements, New Goals and New Measures for Nationally Determined Contributions*, https://unfccc.int/sites/default/files/NDC/2022-06/China's%20Achievements%2C%20New%20Goals%20and%20New%20Measures%20for%20Nationally%20Determined%20Contributions.pdf.

PRC Ministry of Ecology & Environment (MEE) (2017). *Huang Runqiu Speaks at the Founding Ceremony of Lancang-Mekong Environmental Cooperation Center*, https://english.mee.gov.cn/About_MEE/leaders_of_mee/hrq/activities_9795/201802/t20180228_431911.shtml [https://perma.cc/XLZ8-R5ZW].

PRC MEE (2023). *China's Policies and Actions for Addressing Climate Change*, https://www.mee.gov.cn/ywgz/ydqhbh/wsqtkz/202310/W020231027674250657087.pdf.

PRC Ministry of Foreign Affairs (MFA) (2021). *Foreign Ministry Spokesperson Zhao Lijian's Regular Press Conference on June 22, 2021*, www.mfa.gov.cn/eng/xw/fyrbt/lxjzh/202405/t20240530_11347069.html [https://perma.cc/HD82-9AF4].

PRC MFA (2023). *The Global Security Initiative Concept Paper*, http://en.chinadiplomacy.org.cn/pdf/The_Global_Security_Initiative_Concept_Paper.pdf.

PRC State Council (2005). *Decision of the State Council on Implementing Scientific Outlook on Development and Strengthening Environmental Protection*, https://english.mee.gov.cn/Resources/Policies/policies/Frameworkp1/200712/t20071227_115531.shtml [https://perma.cc/AJ4A-57GY].

PRC State Council Information Office (SCIO) (2021a). *China's International Development Cooperation in the New Era*, https://english.www.gov.cn/archive/whitepaper/202101/10/content_WS5ffa6bbbc6d0f72576943922.html [https://perma.cc/Q567-M2WR].

PRC SCIO (2021b). *Biodiversity Conservation in China*, https://english.mee.gov.cn/Resources/publications/Whitep/202110/P020211008419847485077.pdf.

PRC SCIO (2023). *China's Green Development in the New Era*, https://english.www.gov.cn/archive/whitepaper/202301/19/content_WS63c8c053c6d0a757729e5db7.html [https://perma.cc/B935-6MW9].

Qi, J. J. & P. Dauvergne (2022). China's Rising Influence on Climate Governance: Forging a Path for the Global South, *Global Environmental Change*, 73, 102484.

Qin, T. (2020). The Evolution and Challenges in China's Implementation of the Convention on Biological Diversity: A New Analytical Framework, *Int Environ Agreements*, 21(8), 347–365.

Qiu, H.F. (Aug. 13, 2024). Top-level Design Document for Accelerating Comprehensive Green Transformation of Economic and Social Development has Been Released to Further Promote Green and Low-carbon Development (*jiakuai jingji shehui fazhan quanmian lüse zhuanxing dingceng sheji wenjian fabu shenru tuijin lüse ditan fazhan*), *People's Daily*, https://www.gov.cn/zhengce/202408/content_6967932.htm [https://perma.cc/CWM8-9W7D].

Quang, N. M. & J. W. Borton (2023). Revisiting Environmental Security in the Mekong Region, *Heinrich Böll Stiftung*, https://th.boell.org/en/2023/04/10/revisiting-environmental-security-mekong-region.

Quimbre, F., et al. (2023). Global Energy Interconnection: Exploring the Security Implications of a Power Grid Developed and Governed by China, *Rand*, www.rand.org/pubs/research_reports/RRA2490-1.html.

Rigby, M., et al. (2019). Increase in CFC-11 Emissions from Eastern China based on Atmospheric Observations, *Nature* 569, 546-560.

Rodenbiker, J. (2023a). *Ecological States: Politics of Science and Nature in Urbanizing China*, Cornell University Press.

Rodenbiker, J. (2023b). Ecological Civilization Goes Global: China's Green Soft Power and South-South Environmental Initiatives, *Wilson Center*, www.wilsoncenter.org/publication/ecological-civilization-goes-global-chinas-green-soft-power-and-south-south.

Ross, L. (1992). The Politics of Environmental Policy in the People's Republic of China, *Policy Studies Journal*, 20(4), 628–642.

Ross, L. (1998). China: Environmental Protection, Domestic Policy Trends, Patterns of Participation in Regimes and Compliance with International Norms, *China Quarterly*, 156, 809–835.

Ross, L. & M. Silk (1987). *Environmental Law and Policy in the People's Republic of China*, Praeger.

Rudd, K. (2020). The New Geopolitics of China's Climate Leadership, *Asia Society Policy Institute*, https://asiasociety.org/policy-institute/new-geopolitics-chinas-climate-leadership.

Schreurs, M. (2009). *Environmental Politics in Japan, Germany, and the United States*, Cambridge University Press.

Shapiro, J. (2001). *Mao's War Against Nature: Politics and the Environment in Revolutionary China*, Cambridge University Press.

Silver, L., et al. (2022a). Negative Views of China Tied to Critical Views of Its Policies on Human Rights, *Pew Research Center*, www.pewresearch.org/global/2022/06/29/negative-views-of-china-tied-to-critical-views-of-its-policies-on-human-rights/.

Silver, L., et al. (2022b). How Global Public Opinion of China has Shifted in the Xi Era, *Pew Research Center*, www.pewresearch.org/global/2022/09/28/how-global-public-opinion-of-china-has-shifted-in-the-xi-era/.

Silver, L., et al. (2023). Comparing Views of the U.S. and China in 24 Countries, *Pew Research Center*, www.pewresearch.org/global/2023/11/06/comparing-views-of-the-us-and-china-in-24-countries/.

Silver, L., et al. (2024). Most People in 35 Countries Say China Has a Large Impact on Their National Economy, *Pew Research Center*, www.pewresearch.org/global/2024/07/09/most-people-in-35-countries-say-china-has-a-large-impact-on-their-national-economy/.

Simons, C. (2013). *The Devouring Dragon: How China's Rise Threatens Our Natural World*, St. Martin's Press.

Shi, J. (Dec. 2, 2020). China Faces Uphill Struggle to Win over Mekong Neighbours, *South China Morning Post*, https://www.scmp.com/news/china/diplomacy/article/3112292/china-faces-uphill-struggle-win-over-mekong-neighbours.

Smil, V. (1984). *The Bad Earth: Environmental Degradation in China*, Routledge.

Sun, X. & R. Ferris (2018). The Kigali Amendment and China's Critical Roles in Evolving the Montreal Protocol, *Institute for Governance & Sustainable Development*, www.igsd.org/publications/the-kigali-amendments-and-chinas-critical-roles-in-evolving-the-montreal-protocol/.

Sun, Y. & B. Yu (2023). Greening China's Belt and Road Initiative: From Norm Localization to Norm Subsidiarity? *Global Environmental Politics*, 23(1), 1–26.

Sustainable Bus (Apr. 22, 2025). Santiago de Chile Aims to Introduce 1,800 E-Buses This Year (thus Achieving 68% Zero Emission Bus Fleet), https://www.sustainable-bus.com/news/santiago-chile-1800-electric-buses-2025/.

Teng, F. & P. Wang (2021). The Evolution of Climate Governance in China: Drivers, Features, and Effectiveness, *Environmental Politics*, 30(sup1), 141-161.

Tsang, B., et al. (2023). Follow the Money: Chinese Climate-Related Finance to the Global South, *E3G*, www.e3g.org/publications/follow-the-money-chinese-climate-related-finance-to-the-global-south/.

Tsavo Trust (2025). How the SGR Railway Affects Elephants, https://tsavotrust.org/how-the-sgr-railway-affects-elephants/.

UN Environment Programme (UNEP) (2016). *Green is Gold: The Strategy and Actions of China's Ecological Civilization*, https://reliefweb.int/report/china/green-gold-strategy-and-actions-chinas-ecological-civilization.

Urrutia-Mosquera, J. & L. Flórez-Calderón (2024). Characteristics of Potential Buyers of Low-Pollution Vehicles: the Case of Santiago, Chile, *Cogent Social Sciences*, 10(1), 1–18.

U.S. Dept. of Interior, U.S. Geological Survey (USGS) (2025). *Mineral Commodity Summaries 2025*, https://pubs.usgs.gov/periodicals/mcs2025/mcs2025.pdf.

U.S. Dept. of State (2020). Launch of the Mekong-US Partnership: Expanding US Engagement with the Mekong Region, *US Embassy in Cambodia*, https://kh.usembassy.gov/launch-of-the-mekong-u-s-partnership-expanding-u-s-engagement-with-the-mekong-region/.

U.S. Trade Representative (USTR) (2024). *2023 Report to Congress on China's WTO Compliance*, https://ustr.gov/sites/default/files/USTR%20Report%20on%20China's%20WTO%20Compliance%20(Final).pdf.

U.S. White House (2014). *U.S.-China Joint Announcement on Climate Change*, https://obamawhitehouse.archives.gov/the-press-office/2014/11/11/us-china-joint-announcement-climate-change.

U.S. White House (2015). *U.S.-China Joint Presidential Statement on Climate Change*, https://obamawhitehouse.archives.gov/the-press-office/2015/09/25/us-china-joint-presidential-statement-climate-change.

U.S. White House (2016). *U.S.-China Joint Presidential Statement on Climate Change*, https://obamawhitehouse.archives.gov/the-press-office/2016/03/31/us-china-joint-presidential-statement-climate-change.

U.S. White House (2018). *How China's Economic Aggression Threatens the Technologies and Intellectual Property of the United States and the World*, https://trumpwhitehouse.archives.gov/wp-content/uploads/2018/06/FINAL-China-Technology-Report-6.18.18-PDF.pdf.

U.S. White House (2024). *Statement from President Biden on Addressing National Security Risks to the U.S. Auto Industry*, https://bidenwhitehouse.archives.gov/briefing-room/statements-releases/2024/02/29/statement-from-president-biden-on-addressing-national-security-risks-to-the-u-s-auto-industry/.

U.S. White House (2025). *Ending the Green New Scam*, www.whitehouse.gov/wp-content/uploads/2025/05/Ending-the-Green-New-Scam-Fact-Sheet.pdf.

U.S.-China Economic and Security Review Commission (UESRC) (2022). *Hearing on China's Energy Plans and Practices*, www.uscc.gov/hearings/chinas-energy-plans-and-practices.

U.S.-China Economic and Security Review Commission (UESRC) (2022). *Hearing on China's Energy Plans and Practices*, www.uscc.gov/hearings/chinas-energy-plans-and-practices.

van der Kamp, D. (2020). Blunt Force Regulation and Bureaucratic Control: Understanding China's War on Pollution, *Governance*, 34(1), 191–209.

Wang, A. (2011). Green Litigation in China Today, *Dialogue Earth*, https://dialogue.earth/en/pollution/4413-green-litigation-in-china-today/.

Wang, A. (2013). The Search for Sustainable Legitimacy: Environmental Law and Bureaucracy in China, *Harvard Environmental Law Review*, 37, 365–440.

Wang, A. (2018a). Explaining Environmental Information Disclosure in China, *Ecology Law Quarterly*, 44, 865–923.

Wang, A. (2018b). Symbolic Legitimacy and Chinese Environmental Reform, *Environmental Law*, 48(4), 699–760.

Wang, B. (2020). *China's Transition on Climate Change Communication and Governance: From Zero to Hero*, Springer.

Wang, Y. (2022). Beijing's Green Fist: How Environmental Policy Became a Tool of State Control, *Human Rights Watch*, www.hrw.org/news/2022/03/29/beijings-green-fist.

Wang, Y., et al. (2024). No More Coal Abroad! Unpacking the Drivers of China's Green Shift in Overseas Energy Finance, *Energy Research & Social Science*, 111, 103456, www.sciencedirect.com/science/article/pii/S2214629624000471.

Wang-Kaeding, H. (2021). *China's Environmental Foreign Relations*, Routledge.

Wendt, A. (1995). Constructing International Politics, *International Security*, 20(1), 71–81.

Wissenbach, U. & Y. Wang (2017). African Politics Meets Chinese Engineers: The Chinese-Built Standard Gauge Railway Project in Kenya and East Africa, Working Paper No. 2017/13, Johns Hopkins University.

World Bank & PRC Govt. (2007). *Cost of Pollution in China: Economic Estimates of Physical Damages*, https://documents.worldbank.org/en/publication/documents-reports/documentdetail/782171468027560055/cost-of-pollution-in-china-economic-estimates-of-physical-damages.

World Economic Forum (WEF) (2024). Playbook of Solutions: Chile Country Platform, https://initiatives.weforum.org/playbook-of-solutions/chile-country-platform.

Wu, S. S. (2018). The Trouble with the Lancang-Mekong Cooperation Forum, *Diplomat*, https://thediplomat.com/2018/12/the-trouble-with-the-lancang-mekong-cooperation-forum/.

Xi., J. (2017). Xi Jinping Keynote at the World Economic Forum, *CGTN*, https://america.cgtn.com/2017/01/17/full-text-of-xi-jinping-keynote-at-the-world-economic-forum [https://perma.cc/6ZDA-C7YR].

Xi, J. (2021a). Keynote Speech by Chinese President Xi Jinping at the Opening Ceremony of the Boao Forum for Asia Annual Conference 2021, www.fmprc.gov.cn/eng./zy/jj/2020zt/kjgzbdfyyq/202406/t20240606_11379852.html [https://perma.cc/BWJ9-HC72].

Xi, J. (2021b). Remarks by Chinese President Xi Jinping at Leaders Summit on Climate, www.mfa.gov.cn/mfa_eng/xw/zyxw/202504/t20250423_11602660.html [https://perma.cc/4QM9-BR9Z].

Xi, J. (2023). Xi Jinping's speech at the Closing Ceremony of the BRICS Business Forum 2023, https://africa.cgtn.com/full-text-xi-jinpings-speech-at-the-closing-ceremony-of-the-brics-business-forum-2023/ [https://perma.cc/9UL9-BND4].

Xi Jinping Thought on Ecological Civilization Research Center (XJPTECRC) (August 18, 2022). Deeply Study and Implement Xi Jinping Thought on Ecological Civilization, (*shenru xuexi guanche xi jinping shengtai wenming sixiang*), *People's Daily*, http://paper.people.com.cn/rmrb/html/2022-08/18/nw.D110000renmrb_20220818_1-10.htm [https://perma.cc/5YYD-TBXZ].

Xia, Y. (2019). Influence through Infrastructure: Contesting the Chinese-Built Standard Gauge Railway in Kenya, *China Law and Development Research Brief*, No. 9, https://cld.web.ox.ac.uk/files/finalyingxiasgrkenyapdf-0.

Xia, Y. (2024). Environmental Advocacy in a Globalising China: Non-Governmental Organisation Engagement with the Green Belt and Road Initiative, *Journal of Contemporary Asia*, 54(4), 1–23.

Xie, Z. (2020). China's Historical Evolution of Environmental Protection along with the Forty Years' Reform and Opening-Up, *Environmental Science & Ecotechnology*, 1, 100001.

Xinhua (2021). China to Stop Building New Coal-Fired Power Projects Abroad, https://en.people.cn/n3/2021/0922/c90000-9899186.html [https://perma.cc/TWK2-C5KC].

Xinhua (2006). 330,000-Ton (sic) Sand Fell on Beijing, *China Daily*, https://www.chinadaily.com.cn/china/2006-04/19/content_571196.htm [https://perma.cc/FB3H-E9BK].

Xinhua (2022). (Hello Africa). Chinese-built Railway in Harmony with Wildlife Conservation in East Africa, https://english.news.cn/20221214/e16916b45f814c37a2eb6902350e1895/c.html [https://perma.cc/QU56-M4AP].

Yang, S. (2023). Growing Apart: China and India at the Kigali Amendment to the Montreal Protocol, *Global Environmental Politics*, 23(2), 74–101.

Yang, S. (2025). China's Enforcement of International Environmental Agreement: The Case of the Montreal Protocol, *Pacific Basin Law Journal*.

Yeh, E. (2022). The Making of Natural Infrastructure in China's Era of Ecological Civilization, *China Quarterly*, 255, 611–627.

Yeh, E. & E. Loizeaux (2024). China at COP27: CBDR, National Sovereignty, and Climate Justice, *Climate & Development*, 16(10), 906–916.

Zeng, R. (2018). China's Efforts to Protect the Ozone Layer, *Guardian*, www.theguardian.com/environment/2018/aug/05/chinas-efforts-to-protect-the-ozone-layer.

Zhang, Z., et al. (2010). Periodic Climate Cooling Enhanced Natural Disasters and Wars in China During AD 10-1900, *Proceedings of the Royal Society Biological Sciences*, 277, 3745–3753.

Zhao, D. (2009). The Mandate of Heaven and Performance Legitimation in Historical and Contemporary China, *American Behavioral Scientist*, 53(3), 416–433.

Zhao, C., et al. (2009). Verdant Mountains Cannot Stop Water Flowing; Eastward the River Keeps Going, *Xinhua*, www.chinadaily.com.cn/china/2009-12/25/content_9231783.htm [https://perma.cc/VDD3-2S2E].

Zhao, J. & L. Ortolano (2003). The Chinese Government's Role in Implementing Multilateral Environmental Agreements: The Case of the Montreal Protocol, *China Quarterly*, 175, 708–725.

Zhao, Y. & A. Hanson (2024). *Endeavoring for China's Environment and Development Transformation: Three Decades of China Council for International Cooperation on Environment and Development (CCICED)*, Springer.

Zhu, A. L. (2022). *Rosewood*, Harvard University Press.

Zhu, R. (2001). *Report on the Outline of the Tenth Five-Year Plan for National Economic and Social Development*, www.npc.gov.cn/zgrdw/englishnpc/Special_11_5/2010-03/03/content_1690620.htm.

Acknowledgments

I would like to thank C.K. Lee, two anonymous reviewers, Ann Carlson, Kim Clausing, Maximo Langer, Kal Raustiala, Edward Parson, John Delury, Sam Geall, and Shiming Yang for their insightful comments on earlier drafts of this manuscript. This Element has also benefitted tremendously from convenings and conversations with colleagues, including Michael Davidson, Tyler Harlan, Juliet Lu, Jingjing Zhang, my students at UCLA School of Law, and many others. Thank you also to Nick Boroski, Kasper Jastrzebski, Annika Krafcik, Shuhui Guo, Alex Connors, Mary Stachofsky, and Kate Inman for excellent research assistance. This project also benefitted from comments and questions I received during talks at UCLA, UC Berkeley, UC Irvine, Harvard University, the University of Colorado, the Council on Foreign Relations, the University of British Columbia, Victoria University of Wellington (NZ), the University of Arizona, Universidad de Chile, Pontificia Universidad Católica de Chile, Adolfo Ibáñez University (Chile), Peking University, the Chinese Academy of Sciences, Hong Kong University, Duke Kunshan University, PKU Shenzhen Transnational Law School, the Universidad del Pacifico (Peru), and the Association for Asian Studies Annual Conference. This work was supported by funding from UCLA, UCLA School of Law, and the Walter & Shirley Wang Chair in U.S.-China Relations and Communications. This funding also made it possible for this book to be published open access, making the digital version freely available for anyone to read and reuse under a Creative Commons license.

Most of all, I would like to thank Hyeon-Ju Rho and Anna and Benjamin Wang for their patience, support, and advice throughout.

Cambridge Elements

Global China

Ching Kwan Lee
University of California-Los Angeles

Ching Kwan Lee is professor of sociology at the University of California-Los Angeles. Her scholarly interests include political sociology, popular protests, labor, development, political economy, comparative ethnography, China, Hong Kong, East Asia and the Global South. She is the author of three multiple award-winning monographs on contemporary China: Gender and the South China Miracle: Two Worlds of Factory Women (1998), Against the Law: Labor Protests in China's Rustbelt and Sunbelt (2007), and The Specter of Global China: Politics, Labor and Foreign Investment in Africa (2017). Her co-edited volumes include Take Back Our Future: an Eventful Sociology of Hong Kong's Umbrella Movement (2019) and The Social Question in the 21st Century: A Global View (2019).

About the Series

The Cambridge Elements series Global China showcases thematic, region- or country-specific studies on China's multifaceted global engagements and impacts. Each title, written by a leading scholar of the subject matter at hand, combines a succinct, comprehensive and up-to-date overview of the debates in the scholarly literature with original analysis and a clear argument. Featuring cutting edge scholarship on arguably one of the most important and controversial developments in the 21st century, the Global China Elements series will advance a new direction of China scholarship that expands China Studies beyond China's territorial boundaries.

Cambridge Elements

Global China

Elements in the Series

The Hong Kong-China Nexus: A Brief History
John Carroll

Global China as Method
Ivan Franceschini and Nicholas Loubere

Hong Kong: Global China's Restive Frontier
Ching Kwan Lee

China and Global Food Security
Shaohua Zhan

China in Global Health: Past and Present
Mary Augusta Brazelton

Chinese Global Infrastructure
Austin Strange

Global China's Shadow Exchange
Tak-Wing Ngo

Global Civil Society and China
Anthony J. Spires

Global China for Africa's Industrialization?
Carlos Oya

China and the Global Economic Order
Gregory T. Chin, Kevin P. Gallagher

Chinese Global Environmentalism
Alex L Wang

A full series listing is available at: www.cambridge.org/EGLC

For EU product safety concerns, contact us at Calle de José Abascal, 56–1°,
28003 Madrid, Spain or eugpsr@cambridge.org.

www.ingramcontent.com/pod-product-compliance
Lightning Source LLC
LaVergne TN
LVHW011849060526
838200LV00054B/4243